BOOKS AND READERS
IN ANCIENT GREECE
AND ROME

BY

FREDERIC G. KENYON

Late Director and Principal Librarian
of the British Museum

OXFORD
AT THE CLARENDON PRESS
1932

PREFACE

THIS book is the outcome of a course of three lectures which I was invited by the University of London to deliver at King's College in March 1932. The material has been slightly expanded, but the general scale of treatment has not been altered. It does not claim to replace the standard works on ancient book-production, but to supplement them, and that especially with regard to the period during which papyrus was the principal material in use. It is in respect of this period that our knowledge has been chiefly increased in the course of the last two generations through the discoveries of papyri in Egypt. The object of this book is to bring together and make available for students the results of these discoveries. In particular, use has been made of the remarkable collection of papyrus codices recently acquired by Mr. A. Chester Beatty, which has greatly extended our knowledge of this transitional form of book, which appears to have had a special vogue among the Christian community in Egypt.

Although the subject of the book is primarily bibliographical, namely, the methods of book-construction from the date of Homer (whenever that may have been) until the supersession of papyrus by vellum in the fourth century of our era, one of

Preface

its main objects has been to show the bearings of the material and form of books on literary history and criticism, and to consider what new light has been thrown by recent research on the origin and growth of the habit of reading in ancient Greece and Rome.

F. G. K.

August 1932.

CONTENTS

LIST OF ILLUSTRATIONS

I

THE USE OF BOOKS IN ANCIENT GREECE

UNTIL within a comparatively recent period, which may be measured by the lifetime of persons still living, our information with regard to the physical formation and the habitual use of books in ancient Greece and Rome was singularly scanty. Our ancestors were dependent on casual allusions in Greek and Latin authors, intelligible enough to those for whom they were written, but not intended for the information of distant ages, and in no case amounting to formal descriptions. Such results as were obtainable from these sources were gathered together and set out in the well-known handbooks of Birt, Gardthausen, Maunde Thompson, and others. The position, however, has been greatly changed by the discoveries of Greek (and a few Latin) papyri in Egypt during the last half-century. These have not only given us a large number of actual examples of books, ranging from the end of the fourth century B.C. to the seventh century of our era, but have also thrown a good deal of light on the extent of Greek literature surviving in at any rate one province of the Roman Empire, and of the reading habits of the population.

The object of the present book is to present briefly the present state of our knowledge on these

subjects. Some of the information is quite new,
acquired only within the last few months; some is
rather new and has not yet been incorporated in
the existing handbooks; while some has been long
familiar, and only needs to be reconsidered and
restated in the light of the additional evidence.
Much of it will only be interesting to those who
care so much for books as to wish to know something of the details of their construction; but
some of these details also have their value for those
who are concerned with textual criticism. Here
also some previous conceptions have to be revised
in the light of our fuller knowledge.

I propose first to deal with the origins of reading
and the growth of the habit in the Greek world,
from the earliest times to about the third century
after Christ; then to describe the appearance and
methods of manufacture of books during the same
period; next to consider the practice of reading in
the Roman world; and finally to describe the
change which came over the methods of book-
production in the early centuries of the Christian
era, the decline of pagan literature and the growth
of that of Christianity, leading up in the fourth
century to the general adoption of vellum as the
material of books, and the transition from the
ancient world to the Middle Ages. For the earlier
part of the period under consideration, before
about 300 B.C., such additional evidence as we

have comes from the increase of our general knowledge of the ancient world, due to archaeological exploration, and not from concrete examples of actual books. For the later part the discoveries of papyri in Egypt come into play.

Any consideration of Greek literature necessarily begins with the Homeric poems; and in this connexion we have in the first place to take into account what is now known as to the origins of writing in the countries surrounding the eastern Mediterranean. With regard to this subject, it is not too much to say that our knowledge has been revolutionized by modern archaeological discoveries. Only about a generation ago it was accepted doctrine that writing was practically unknown to the Homeric age. In Grote's *History of Greece*, which then held the field, it is laid down in round terms and without qualification that 'neither coined money, nor the art of writing, nor painting, nor sculpture, nor imaginative architecture, belong to the Homeric and Hesiodic times'.[1] Few things, he says, can in his opinion be more improbable than the existence of long written poems in the ninth century before the Christian era. He would rather suppose that a small reading class may have come into existence about the middle of the seventh century, about which time the opening of Egypt to Grecian commerce would furnish increased

[1] Part I, ch. 20 (vol. ii, p. 116, of edition of 1883).

4 *The Use of Books in Ancient Greece*

facilities for obtaining the requisite papyrus to write upon.[1] To that period, accordingly, he would assign the commencement of written literature in Greece.

Here we find ourselves at once at a point on which much evidence is available to us which was unknown to Grote. Recent discoveries in Egypt, in Mesopotamia, in Crete, and in Asia Minor have vastly increased our knowledge of the practice of writing in the ancient world. I will summarize this evidence quite briefly, beginning first with Egypt.[2]

The Prisse Papyrus in the Bibliothèque Nationale at Paris is believed to have been written during the Twelfth Dynasty of Egypt (about 2200–2000 B.C.). It contains two ethical treatises, the Teaching of Kagemna and the Teaching of Ptah-Hetep. According to the colophon at the end of the former of these treatises, Kagemna lived in the reign of Huni, the predecessor of Seneferu, at the end of the Third Dynasty (about 3100 B.C.), and compiled this collection of moral precepts for the benefit of his children. Ptah-Hetep lived a little later, in the reign of King Isesi, or Assa, of the Fifth Dynasty (about 2883–2855 B.C.), and his book also was written for his son. We have thus from Egypt an actual manuscript which was

[1] *Ibid.*, pp. 143, 150.
[2] The following paragraph is extracted from a book of my own, *Ancient Books and Modern Discoveries*, issued in a limited edition by the Caxton Club of Chicago in 1927.

written before the end of the third millennium B.C., and the works contained in it, if we are to believe their own statements, were composed respectively in the fourth millennium and early in the third. Nor is there any reason to doubt these statements; for there is confirmatory evidence. The Book of the Dead, of which we have manuscripts on papyrus dating from the Eighteenth Dynasty (about 1580–1320 B.C.) and portions written in ink on wooden coffins of the Eleventh Dynasty or earlier,[1] certainly existed many centuries earlier, since the so-called Pyramid recension is found carved in the pyramids of Unas, the last king of the Fifth Dynasty, and of Teta and Pepi I of the Sixth Dynasty. It is not unreasonable to suppose that these texts must have been written on some more ephemeral material before being carved on stone. Egyptian tradition would carry them back even further still. A chapter is said to have been 'found' in the reign of Semti of the First Dynasty; and the same king's name is associated with a recipe in a book of medicine which was apparently written or edited in his reign. Further, King Zoser, of the Third Dynasty, is said to have been a patron of literature, and portraits and tombs of persons described as 'scribes' exist from the Fourth Dynasty. Certain chapters of the Book of the Dead are said to have been composed in the reign of

[1] Coffins of Amamu and Mentu-Hetep in the British Museum.

Men-kau-ra (Mycerinus), the fifth king of that
Dynasty, and the medical prescriptions preserved
in British Museum Papyrus 10059 are assigned to
the Fifth Dynasty. The practice of writing is
therefore well attested for Egypt at least as far
back as the third millennium B.C.

From Mesopotamia we have evidence of the use
of writing of at least equal antiquity, and a much
greater wealth of actual specimens. The archives
discovered by the American excavators at Nippur
in 1888–1900 include tablets bearing literary texts
(notably the Sumerian version of the Deluge story)
which are assigned to about 2100 B.C. or earlier.[1]
A fragment of the same narrative, previously discovered, bears an actual date equivalent to 1967
B.C. The texts themselves, being in the Sumerian
language, must have been composed much earlier.
Nor would there have been any difficulty about
recording them in writing; for the evidence of the
existence of cuneiform writing now goes back well
into the fourth millennium. Thousands of tablets

---

[1] My former colleague, Mr. C. J. Gadd, in confirming this
dating, suggests that though the compositions contained in these
tablets are doubtless older, they may not have been committed to
writing so long as the population and language of the country
were predominantly Sumerian. The establishment of the Isin
and Larsa dynasties at about this time marks the definite passing
of the land to Semitic predominance and language, and it
became necessary that the old and difficult Sumerian literature
should be written down. Translations into Semitic begin to
appear at about the same time.

discovered at Telloh, at Ur, and at Warka show that writing was in constant use for the preservation of accounts, contracts, business archives, foundation tablets, building records, and other purposes of daily life throughout the whole of the third millennium B.C. and probably earlier. Writing was therefore available for literary purposes as early as it was wanted; but to what extent it was actually used there is at present no evidence to determine.

From the Hittite Empire also, which dominated eastern Asia Minor in the second millennium, we have ample evidence of the use of writing. The archives of Boghaz-keui contain the records of the Hittite sovereigns, written in both Semitic and Hittite dialects in Babylonian cuneiform. These have only recently been deciphered and some progress made in the interpretation of the Hittite language. As will be seen presently, they have a direct bearing on the Homeric question; but in any case they are decisive evidence of the habitual use of writing at this period. There is also writing in Hittite hieroglyphics, but they have not yet been deciphered.

Coming yet nearer to the Greek world, we have the Cretan tablets discovered by Sir Arthur Evans at Knossos. These are in two forms of script, pictographic and linear. They have not yet been deciphered, but certainly include accounts. So far as is at present known, there are no literary texts among them; but they prove the existence and free use of writing in Crete at least as far back as 2000 B.C.

It is therefore now amply proved that writing was in habitual use in Mesopotamia, in Egypt, in Asia Minor, and by the Minoan predecessors of the Greeks in Crete at dates far preceding the beginnings of Greek literature; and the question naturally arises, Is it likely that a people such as the Greeks, of lively intelligence, of ready initiative, and with literary tastes, would have remained ignorant, or have made no use, of an invention currently practised among their neighbours, and even their Minoan ancestors, and of such obvious utility for their own purposes? The natural presumption must clearly be to the contrary.

Two objections may possibly be made at this point. First it may be asked how it is that no specimens of early writing have survived in Greece, as they have in the adjoining countries that have been mentioned. The answer is that the Greeks did not use baked clay tablets, as did the Sumerians, Babylonians, Hittites, and Cretans, while skins and papyrus, which they did use in later times, and which must be taken to be the materials which they would naturally have used in earlier times, could not survive in the Greek climate and soil, as they have survived in the drier soil and climate of Egypt. It has further been argued that if the early Greeks had been acquainted with the practice of writing, some trace of it would have survived in the form of inscriptions on stone. This is an argument which may any day be invalidated by new discoveries; but in any case it is far from being conclusive. No inscriptions have so far been discovered among the extensive remains of Minoan Crete; yet we know from the isolated discovery of the archives of Knossos by Sir Arthur Evans that the Minoans were familiar with the use of writing. The absence of inscriptions is therefore not a valid argument against an acquaintance with letters on the part of the Mycenaean Greeks; and the presumption to the contrary, based on the general use of writing in the countries around the eastern Mediterranean, appears to hold good.

Let us look now at the earliest remains of Greek literature, and consider the probabilities as to the method of their composition and preservation.

Fifty years ago the Homeric and Hesiodic poems stood out by themselves as an island, separated by a gulf of centuries from the mainland of Greek literature; and the Trojan war and all the traditional early history of Greece were regarded as legendary, down to about the time of Solon. Now, as the result of the discoveries of the last fifty years, the gaps in our knowledge are being filled up, the origins of Greece are being brought into connexion with the histories of the surrounding countries, and we are beginning to form a general picture of the whole course of development in the countries around the eastern Mediterranean. We know that there was a great civilization in Crete in the third and second millennia, which came to an abrupt end, while still in great splendour, in the fourteenth century. We know that the civilization to which we give the name Mycenaean was a descendant and offshoot from the Minoan stem, and out of this, after the break caused by the Dorian invasion, comes the full Hellenic culture which we know. Further, we have lately learnt from the Hittite records, now being painfully interpreted, that contemporaneously with the Hittite Empire of about 1300–1200 B.C. there was a considerable power on both sides of the Aegean whose princes and dominions bore names in which we can recognize names familiar to us in Greek history and legend—Eteocles, Aegeus, Achaeans, Lesbos, and so on.[1] The general tendency in this, as in other provinces of knowledge, is to vindicate tradition, as containing at least a substantial modicum of truth. Let us consider therefore the Greek traditions as to both facts and dates.

Greek tradition assigned the origin of Greek

[1] Forrer's equations of Greek and Hittite forms of names, though possibly open to question in detail (as to which I am not competent to judge), seem to me too striking and too numerous to justify disbelief in general.

literature to the introduction of the alphabet by
Cadmus from Phoenicia; and the traditional date
of Cadmus is about 1350–1300. The traditional
date of the fall of Troy is 1184 or 1183 B.C., and
this accords sufficiently well with the indications
of the Hittite records. The traditional dates for
Homer vary from 1075 to about 875. Clinton
accepts an intermediate date, about 975, which
is that favoured by Aristotle. The latest writer on
the subject, Mr. Bowra, after saying that 'the statement of Herodotus that he lived in the latter part
of the ninth century and was a contemporary of
Hesiod may not be far from the truth', proceeds
in the next sentence to place him late in the eighth
century. The latter date is surely too late, and
is perhaps merely a slip of the pen: for there is
good evidence for placing Arctinus, the author of
the *Aethiopis*, in the first half of that century
(*c.* 775–750); and if one thing is more certain than
another, it is that the *Iliad* and *Odyssey* preceded
the poems of the Epic Cycle.

If, then, we take the ninth century as the latest
date for Homer which suits the evidence,[1] what
sort of picture can we make of the manner of the

[1] It might have been wiser to imitate the prudence of Pausanias:
'Though I have investigated very carefully the dates of Hesiod
and Homer, I do not like to state my results, knowing as I do the
carping disposition of some people, especially of the professors of
poetry at the present day' (ix. 30. 3, Frazer's transl.). But it
could hardly be avoided.

formation and preservation of his poems? (I am
assuming that there was a personal Homer, who
was mainly responsible for both *Iliad* and *Odyssey*;
but those who prefer the older view, now less,
prevalent than it once was, that they are the work
of a syndicate, or grew by themselves out of a
number of detached lays, botched together by an
incompetent editor, have only to substitute the
phrase 'the Homeric poems' for 'Homer'.) As
I have already shown, there is no *a priori* reason
why they should not have been written down.
Writing had been in common use for centuries in
the lands adjoining the Aegean and Mediterranean
on the east; and if Cadmus or any one else introduced writing to Greece about the fourteenth
century, that gives plenty of time for the establishment of the practice, and for the production of
those earlier efforts in verse which must surely have
preceded the consummate technique of Homer.

Looking at the matter from the point of view of
internal probability, the argument for a written
Homer appears to me overwhelmingly strong. It
is difficult even to conceive how poems on such
a scale could have been produced without the
assistance of written copies. It is not that the feat
of memorizing poems of such length is incredible.
On the contrary, one of the speakers in Xenophon's
Symposium[1] says that his father compelled him to

[1] *Symp.* iii. 5.

learn the whole of the Homeric poems, and that
he could still recite the entire *Iliad* and *Odyssey*.
Parallels are quoted from various primitive peoples;
and it is on record that in the nineteenth century
one young Wykehamist (afterwards the defender
of Silistria in the Crimean War) learnt the whole
of the *Iliad*, and another the whole of the *Aeneid*,
in the days when such feats of memory were encouraged at Winchester.[1] The poems, once composed, could have been recited; but could they
have been carried in the memory of the poet during the process of composition? And are we to
picture the poet, after completing his *magnum opus*,
as assembling a corps of rhapsodists around him,
and reciting his work over and over to them until
they had committed it to memory? It is difficult
to believe. And if there was one original author's
copy, why should not each rhapsodist, or at any
rate each school of rhapsodists, have possessed one
also? It seems easier to believe this than the
contrary.

Moreover, even if we are prepared to believe
that Homer and the Homeridae could have composed and memorized the Homeric poems without
book, what are we to say of Hesiod? Rhapsodists
might indeed think it worth while to learn the
Catalogoi, which contained the popular legends of
the gods and heroes, and for which listeners could

---

[1] Leach, *History of Winchester College*, p. 427.

readily be found; but can we suppose that there would have been much of a public for the *Works and Days*, with its combination of a purely personal quarrel with agricultural precepts? It seems to me incredible that such a poem should have survived unless it had been written down, whether on lead, as shown to Pausanias on Helicon, or in some other fashion. The same might perhaps be said of the poems of the Epic Cycle. The poets who produced them must have been familiar with the *Iliad* and *Odyssey*, not only generally but in detail. They must have been rhapsodists themselves or habitual frequenters of rhapsodists; and they must have acquired corps of rhapsodists to learn their own poems in turn and recite them. But Hesiod was either the contemporary of Homer, as was held by many in antiquity, or not much later; and the later one brings down Homer, the nearer he comes to the earliest of the Cyclic poets. And if the works of Hesiod and the Cyclics were written down, it is surely straining at a gnat to refuse to allow the same to Homer. Now that the general antiquity of writing in the world of the Homeric age is established, it is impossible to maintain that writing was practised in the Greek lands in the seventh and eighth centuries, but could not have been known in the ninth, or even earlier. The basis for the old belief is cut away.

I believe therefore that sober criticism must

allow that the *Iliad* and *Odyssey* were composed in writing, and that written copies of them existed to assist the rhapsodists who recited them and to control their variations. It is much more difficult, however, to say what was the form of these written copies, or in what manner they circulated. There is no evidence of the existence of anything that can be called a reading public. I do not attach any importance to the fact that writing is not mentioned in Homer, except in the reference to the σήματα λυγρά carried by Bellerophon. There was little occasion for the mention of it in such poems of war and adventure; and I do not think it would be difficult to find modern poems, describing a primitive age, which are equally devoid of references to it. But we do have references to the recital of poetry, and if reading had been a common practice, we might have found some allusion to it. At any rate, without evidence which we certainly have not, I do not think we are entitled to assume its existence.[1]

---

[1] Hesiod emphasizes the charm of literature, but it is poetry recited, not read (*Theog.* 98–103):

εἰ γάρ τις καὶ πένθος ἔχων νεοκηδέϊ θυμῷ
ἄζηται κραδίην ἀκαχήμενος, αὐτὰρ ἀοιδὸς
Μουσάων θεράπων κλεῖα προτέρων ἀνθρώπων
ὑμνήσῃ, μάκαράς τε θεοὺς οἳ Ὄλυμπον ἔχουσιν,
αἶψ' ὅ γε δυσφρονέων ἐπιλήθεται, οὐδέ τι κηδέων
μέμνηται· ταχέως δὲ παρέτραπε δῶρα θεάων.

This is consistent with the theory that, while writing was employed for the composition and preservation of literature, the normal method of publication was by recital.

I imagine, therefore, that written copies of poems, though they existed, were rare, and were the property of professional reciters, from whom alone the general public derived their knowledge of them. On what material they were written it is impossible to say. Papyrus would have been obtainable from Egypt, and we know from Herodotus that skins were used at an early date in Asia Minor; but beyond that we cannot go, in the present state of our knowledge. It is, however, fairly certain that poems of such length, whether written on skins or on papyrus, could not have existed in single volumes, but must have occupied a number of separate rolls. Such a division into rolls might naturally lead to the division into books with which we are familiar. As will be seen later, a book of Thucydides corresponds with the contents of a papyrus roll of the largest size in ordinary use; and the natural presumption is that the twenty-four books of the *Iliad* represent a stage in its history when it occupied twenty-four rolls. When this division was made is unknown; but it may be worth observing that this theory of its origin would appear to point to a date earlier than the Alexandrian age. From that age we possess a number of specimens of Homeric manuscripts, and it is clear that a normal roll could easily accommodate two books of the *Iliad*. It would seem, therefore, that the division into twenty-four

A POETESS WITH TABLETS AND STYLUS

books may go back to a period when rolls were shorter or handwritings larger; in which connexion it may be observed that the earliest extant literary papyrus (that of Timotheus's *Persae*, of the end of the 4th cent. B.C.) is in a much larger hand than later manuscripts. The *Odyssey* could, of course, easily have been written in fewer rolls than the *Iliad*, but the division into twenty-four books was obviously made to correspond.

While on the subject of the tradition of the Homeric poems, it may be permissible to refer to a phenomenon, of which there is considerable evidence among the papyri of the third century B.C., namely the existence of copies containing a considerable number of additional lines, which do not appear in our standard text. These lines are not substantial additions to the narrative of the poems, but are rather of the nature of verbal padding. There is no reason to regard them as authentic, and it is easy to account for their existence. When copies were scarce and means of inter-comparison almost non-existent, it would have been easy for a rhapsodist who fancied himself as an inventor of Homeric phrases to produce an edition of his own, which might obtain local currency. Only when copies from various sources were brought together in a single place, as at Alexandria, was comparative criticism possible, and then such excrescences as these were speedily

removed. They are rare in papyri of the second
century B.C., and unknown later.

With the beginning of the seventh century, or
possibly a few years earlier, we reach the lyric
age of Greek poetry, when the circulation of literature must be taken definitely to have passed from
the rhapsodes to manuscripts. The recitations
of the rhapsodes, at least of the Homeric poems,
no doubt continued to be a feature of the Pan-
hellenic festivals; and the setting of poems to
music, as in the case of the odes of Terpander or
Alcman, or later the epinician odes and dithyrambs
of Pindar, Simonides, and Bacchylides, provided a
new form of publicity for the poets. But the more
personal compositions, such as the satires of Archi-
lochus, the political verses of Solon, and many of
the lyrics of Sappho and Alcaeus, were quite un-
fitted for musical accompaniment or public performance, and must have circulated, so far as they
circulated at all, in manuscript. Throughout the
seventh and sixth centuries the circumstances must
have been very much the same. Poems, epic,
elegiac, and lyric, were being produced in considerable quantities. The poets were acquainted
with one another's works, and enjoyed reputations
among their contemporaries. Their poems must
have been written down, and must have been
accessible to those who desired them: but we have
no evidence to give precision to our picture of the

methods of publication. Lyric and elegiac poems, each composed for a particular purpose, may often have circulated singly; but whether their authors gathered them together into collected editions we do not know. Later, we know that they were so gathered; that the odes of Alcaeus formed six volumes,[1] that Sappho's were arranged in nine,[2] that the epinicia, dithyrambs, and paeans of Pindar and Bacchylides were brought together in separate groups; but we do not know that this arrangement was made in the lifetimes of the respective poets, and it is more likely to be attributable to the scholars of Alexandria. An organized book-trade at this time is highly improbable: at the same time it is evident that copies of the works of all these poets must have existed and have circulated in sufficient numbers to secure their continued preservation, and to make it possible for them to be gathered into libraries when libraries came into being.

In the fifth century we reach the culminating point of Greek literature, with Pindar, Simonides, and Aeschylus in its earlier portions, followed by Sophocles and Euripides, Herodotus and Thucydides, Aristophanes and his rivals in comedy, and

[1] Suidas, s.v.
[2] So Suidas, s.v. Lobel (Σαπφοῦς Μέλη, Oxford, 1925) suggests that the true number may be eight, and that the division may be Attic, not Alexandrian. But it seems more in accord with the Alexandrian type of mind.

all the great band of poets and prose writers who survive for us only in quotations and allusions. It is a period of intense literary creativeness on the highest scale, and yet, so far as we can judge, of very limited book-production. Oral methods of publicity continued. The odes of the ceremonial lyrists were no doubt produced with musical accompaniment on the occasions for which they were written; the tragedies and comedies were performed on the stage; even the works of the historians may have been read at the great festivals, as that of Herodotus is said to have been. It stands to reason that even for these purposes a certain amount of production in manuscript form was necessary. The performers must have had copies from which they learnt their parts; the authors and reciters must have had their copies to read from. What is to some extent doubtful is the circulation of copies of books among the general public, and the growth of a habit of reading.

Contemporary references to the reading of books are very rare during the golden age of Greek literature. In Plato's *Phaedo* Socrates is represented as referring to a volume of Anaxagoras, which he heard read and subsequently procured; and in the *Apology* he says that copies of Anaxagoras could be bought by any one for a drachma.[1] In the

---

[1] *Phaedo*, 97 b, 98 b (in the latter passage the plural, τὰς

Theaetetus Eucleides of Megara recalls a conversation between Socrates and Theaetetus which he wrote down at the time, and which he now causes a slave to read aloud to himself and his companion.[1] In the *Phaedrus*, on the other hand, Socrates speaks contemptuously of a dependence upon books in comparison with memory;[2] and his attitude is the same in his conversation with Euthydemus recorded by Xenophon.[3] More valuable for our present purpose is the statement of Xenophon's Socrates that he was accustomed to unroll the treasures of the sages of old time which they had left in books written by them, and to study and make extracts from them with his friends.[4] This proves the existence of the practice of consulting books in a study or library; but it must be admitted that the general picture which we have, both in Plato and in Xenophon, is of oral instruction and conversation, not of reading and private study.

It would be a mistake, however, to overstress this scantiness of evidence as an argument against

[1] *Theaet.* 143 a, b.

[2] *Phaedr.* 274 e ff. Books may be useful to refresh the memory, but are greatly inferior to the spoken word as a means of education (ibid. 276 d). Similarly Isocrates (*Phil.* 25–7) admits the inferiority of the written to the spoken word.

[3] Xen. *Mem.* iv. ii.

[4] Ibid. i. vi. 14: τοὺς θησαυροὺς τῶν πάλαι σοφῶν ἀνδρῶν οὓς ἐκεῖνοι κατέλιπον ἐν βιβλίοις γράψαντες, ἀνελίττων κοινῇ σὺν τοῖς

the existence and even the abundant existence and free use of books in the latter part of the fifth century. The very casualness of these allusions is a proof that there was nothing extraordinary about them, and that the accessibility of books might be taken for granted. A minute acquaintance with Homer was assumed as part of the equipment of every educated man, and allusions to Hesiod, to the Cyclic poets, or to the lyrists are made with an assurance which implies that they would be understood. Aristophanes has a verbal knowledge of the works of Aeschylus and Euripides which could not have been derived from stage representation alone. Thucydides knew and refers to the works of his predecessors in history; and the works of the physical philosophers and of the medical schools that followed Hippocrates could only have been known through circulation in manuscripts. Euthydemus, the younger contemporary of Socrates, possessed while still quite young a collection of the works of the best poets and philosophers:[1] and the cheapness and ready accessibility of the works of Anaxagoras, referred to above, cannot have been confined to that philosopher.

More illuminating, perhaps, is a line in the *Frogs* of Aristophanes, in which the chorus, inciting the rival poets to bring their wares to the test, assures them that they need have no fear lest the audience

----

[1] Xen. *Mem.* IV. ii. I.

should be unable to follow and appreciate them (as had apparently been the case at the first performance of the play); for they are *now* all men who have seen the world in the course of their military service, and each of them has his own copy of the play in his hand and can understand the points.[1] This seems to imply that a certain amount of book-knowledge of literature could now be presumed, though formerly it was not the case. And this is the general conclusion to which all the evidence seems to point.

A final reference may be made to a passage in Xenophon's *Anabasis*, where among the cargoes of ships wrecked near Salmydessus, on the north coast of Asia Minor, 'many books' (πολλαὶ βίβλοι) are said to have been included.[2]

Of the formation of libraries there is practically no evidence. Athenaeus,[3] at a much later date, does indeed refer to traditional libraries formed by Pisistratus and Polycrates of Samos in the sixth century, but these are separated by two and a half centuries from the next collections that he can

---

[1] Arist. *Ran.* 1114, βιβλίον τ' ἔχων ἕκαστος μανθάνει τὰ δεξιά. The use of the singular seems to imply a single roll which the spectator could have with him in the theatre, not the collected works of Aeschylus and Euripides, which would of course occupy many rolls. But whatever be the exact explanation, it is implied that the younger generation is accustomed to the use of books. I have to thank Mr. F. R. Earp for calling my attention to this passage.

[2] Xen. *Anab.* vii. 5, 14 (quoted by Sandys, *History of Classical Scholarship*, i. 84).   [3] *Deipnosophistae*, i. 4.

mention, and may be little more than mythical. His next example is Eucleides, who may be identical with the Megarian philosopher already referred to, though Athenaeus calls him an Athenian. His list also includes the name of Euripides. These libraries, however, like that owned by Euthydemus, as mentioned above, would have been small private collections of books, amounting at most to a few score rolls; and even they seem to have been exceptional.

The general conclusion would therefore seem to be that at the end of the fifth century and in the early part of the fourth, books existed in Athens in considerable quantity, and were cheap and easily accessible. A habit of reading was growing up, but was not yet very firmly established. The general opinion did not rate reading highly as a means of mental training, in comparison with the play of mind upon mind in oral discussion. The lively Athenian mind accepted Bacon's distinction, and preferred the ready man to the full man. The age of the full man was, however, approaching.

When we pass on another stage, from the generation of Plato to that of Aristotle, a very distinct change is marked. Whereas in the earlier period, while books must have been produced in considerable numbers, a reading public could hardly be said to exist, we have now reached a period of readers and libraries. Even if it were not actually

related that Aristotle possessed a library, the fate
of which after his death is on record,[1] it would be
obvious from the mere list of his works that it
must have been so. His great compilations,
whether of physical science or of political constitu-
tions, could not have been produced without a
reference library; and his practice set an example
which was followed by his disciples, such as
Theophrastus and Menon, and which profoundly
influenced the course of Greek literary history.
It is not too much to say that with Aristotle
the Greek world passed from oral instruction
to the habit of reading. The history of libraries
in the Greek and Graeco-Roman world is rightly
taken to start with the foundation of the Museum
at Alexandria; but the foundation of the Museum
and of the great Alexandrian Library was made
possible by the change of habit which took form
in the time, and largely under the influence, of
Aristotle.

From the date of the foundation of the Museum
and Library of Alexandria we are at last on firm
ground in dealing with the book-world of Greek
civilization. We have no longer to depend on
deductions from casual allusions or from abstract
probabilities. We have records on a fairly ample

[1] Strabo, xiii. i. 54, where Aristotle is described as πρῶτος ὧν
ἴσμεν συναγαγὼν βιβλία, καὶ διδάξας τοὺς ἐν Αἰγύπτῳ βασιλέας βιβλιο-
θήκης σύνταξιν.

scale; and more than that, we have actual specimens of the books of that period, and know how
they were manufactured, and what they looked
like. The credit of the foundation of these institu-
tions is variously assigned to Ptolemy I (Soter) and
Ptolemy II (Philadelphus). The truth would appear to be that the deliberate collection of books
to form a library and a centre of study was begun
by Ptolemy I, as a step in the hellenization of
Egypt, while the complete establishment of both
Library and Museum was accomplished by Philadelphus. Ptolemy I was himself an author and the
friend of authors, and he entrusted the formation
of the library to Demetrius of Phalerum, a disciple
of Theophrastus and an encyclopaedic writer, who
for ten years had given Athens experience of the
rule of a philosopher-tyrant. Expelled from Athens,
he was glad to find an asylum with Ptolemy (290
B.C.) and to confine himself to the more harmless
task of collecting books.

That books were by this time plentiful is shown
by the size which Ptolemy's library almost immediately attained. According to one account,
200,000 volumes had been collected by the end
of his reign, i.e. within about five years. Such
figures are, however, totally unreliable, and
another story speaks of 100,000 at the death of
Philadelphus, and yet another of 700,000 when
the Library was burnt in the time of Caesar; but

in any case it is clear that a substantial collection was formed by Soter, which was transferred by his son to the Museum of which he was the founder. This 'Temple of the Muses' was the first great library after those formed by the kings of Nineveh; and besides being a library, it was an Academy of Letters and Learning. Eminent men of letters and scholars, such as Callimachus, Apollonius Rhodius, and Aristarchus, were placed in succession at its head; students gathered round it; a corps of copyists was employed to multiply manuscripts; and Alexandria became the centre of the literary life of the Hellenistic world.

We have now reached a state of things which is comparable with our own times. Greek culture had broken the bounds of the old Greek world, had spread over the Near East and the Mediterranean basin, and absorbed Rome as soon as Rome had awakened to intellectual life. The formation of the Alexandrian Library, and of other libraries elsewhere, of which that of Pergamum, to be mentioned later, is the most notable, encouraged the production of books, much as the British Museum Library encourages and facilitates it to-day. The output of books of learning, or of what desired to pass as learning, was enormous. The standard of works of the highest literature might have fallen woefully since the generations of Aeschylus and Thucydides and Plato; but the trade of book-making prospered exceedingly. Commentators, compilers, popularizers swarmed, as they do to-day; and it is evident that there was a great quantity of minor literature which has disappeared with hardly a trace.

In estimating the extent of the habit of reading in the Greek world, we have to remember that the literature in the Greek language which has survived to our own day is only a small fraction of that which existed in the three centuries on either side of the Christian era. It may be of interest to adduce evidence on this head, some of which is the result of recent discoveries.

There are two methods by which some idea could be obtained of the total extent of Greek literature. One is an examination of the references to lost works which appear in authors who still survive. It would be a laborious, but not un-interesting or uninstructive task to compile a cata-logue of lost Greek books from the references to them in extant literature. I can only give a few indications here. We know that, with the excep-tion of a substantial part of Pindar and a smaller fraction of Bacchylides, all Greek lyric poetry has disappeared as a collected whole, and is known to us only through casual quotations. We know that only 7 plays of Aeschylus have survived out of at least 70, only 7 of Sophocles out of 113, only 18 of Euripides out of 92, only 11 of Aristophanes

out of at least 43; and that of all the other tragic
and comic poets of Greece we have nothing. In
the great anthology compiled by Stobaeus about
the end of the fifth century, the quotations from
lost works far exceed those from works that have
survived, although the latter are naturally the
most famous works of their respective authors, and
therefore the most likely to be quoted. A rough
count shows that in the first thirty sections of
Stobaeus, 314 quotations are taken from works
still extant, and 1,115 from works that are lost.
Out of 470 names in Photius's list of authors quoted
by Stobaeus, 40 at most can be said to exist in any
substantial form to-day. And this is from a collection which draws naturally from the best works
and the best authors, and takes no account of the
much larger mass of inferior literature, from which
no quotations are taken, and much of which had
already disappeared at the time when the anthology was made.

An earlier work which consists mainly of extracts is the *Deipnosophistae* of Athenaeus, which as
a rag-bag of quotations may be compared with
Burton's *Anatomy of Melancholy*. I have counted
the quotations or references in a single book, and
(though I cannot guarantee the absolute accuracy
of the enumeration) I find that out of 366 quotations (mainly from the comic dramatists) only 23
are from works that have come down to us. It is

as though of all the works quoted in Burton, only those had survived which are included in the World's Classics or Everyman's Library.

The second line of investigation into the extent of Greek literature is to be found in an examination of the fragments of literary works which have been brought to light among the papyri discovered in such quantities in Egypt during the last fifty years. The vast majority of these fragments are derived from the rubbish heaps that surrounded the towns and villages of Graeco-Roman Egypt, and especially those of Oxyrhynchus. They are the débris of the books which the Greek-reading population of Egypt used and possessed. They are therefore specially valuable for our present purpose. Any scrap of papyrus sufficiently large to make it possible to ascertain the character of its text is evidence of the existence of a complete manuscript at the time when it was written. It is therefore possible for us to determine the proportion between the manuscripts of works that have otherwise come down to us and those which have been lost. We can see, further, what authors were the most popular, and in what centuries there was the greatest activity in the production (and therefore presumably the study) of books.

The latest inventory of literary papyri (including under this term the fragments of vellum manuscripts, tablets, and ostraca which have been found in the same conditions) is~~that of C.~~ H. Oldfather, compiled in 1922.[1] The ten years since that date have added appreciably to the totals, but have not affected the general character of the results. Omitting Biblical texts and Christian works, as forming a category apart, Oldfather lists 1,189 literary manuscripts, represented sometimes by the merest scraps, sometimes by substantial rolls or codices. Of this total, no less than 315, or more than a quarter of the whole, are Homeric, 282 being actual copies of parts of the *Iliad* or *Odyssey*, while 33 are commentaries, lexicons, or the like. Of the remaining 887, 237 are from works which have come down to us otherwise; 650 are from works wholly lost or known to us only by quotations or references. It is fair to add that among these are included a number of school exercises, brief extracts, and some works which are barely on the fringe of literature. Nevertheless the disproportion is marked, and completely confirms the conclusions indicated by the evidence of Stobaeus and Athenaeus. It is clear that the lost works of Greek literature very greatly exceeded in number those which have survived. Every student of the collections of 'fragments' of Greek authors will agree in this conclusion.

It is interesting also, as indicating the literary tastes and educational practice of Graeco-Roman

[1] University of Wisconsin Studies, no. 9 (Madison, 1923).

Egypt, to observe the distribution of the known authors and the dates from which the remains are most numerous. Homer, as already indicated, predominates quite enormously. He was the indispensable subject-matter of education, and just as a knowledge of the Bible is regarded as an essential part of the equipment of every one with any tincture of culture in this country, so it was with Homer in the Greek world. But it is noteworthy that the predominance of the *Iliad* over the *Odyssey* is just as great as the predominance of Homer over all other authors. Of the 282 manuscripts of Homer represented in Oldfather's list, 221 are from the *Iliad,* and only 61 from the *Odyssey.* Of the other great writers, Demosthenes is the most fully represented, with 48 copies of one or other of his orations, besides three commentaries and the more extensive work of Didymus, of which a substantial papyrus exists at Berlin. Next to him, as is only natural, comes Euripides, with 32 manuscripts; and after him Menander, with 26, though the attribution of some of these is doubtful. This, in view of the popularity of Menander and the extent to which his comedies lent themselves to quotation, is only what one would have expected. Since the discovery of the Cairo codex, which contains substantial portions of four comedies, Menander may be reckoned with Bacchylides, Hyperides, Herodas, and Timotheus as an author who has, at least to some considerable extent, been restored to us from the sands of Egypt. To them one should perhaps add Ephorus, if, as seems probable, he is the author of the historical work discovered at Oxyrhynchus, and Aristotle as a historian, in virtue of the 'Αθηναίων πολιτεία. After these follow Plato, with 23 manuscripts, Thucydides with 21, Hesiod with 20 (mostly from the *Catalogues* and the *Theogonia*, only four being copies of the *Works and Days*), Isocrates with 18, Aristophanes and Xenophon with 17 each, Sophocles with 12, and Pindar with 11. That Sappho also retained popularity is shown by the appearance of eight manuscripts, one of which is as late as the seventh century. The most noticeable gaps in the list are Aeschylus, Herodotus, and Aristotle. Aeschylus is represented only by a single fragment, which has been doubtfully assigned to his *Carians* or *Europa*; of his more famous works no trace has been preserved. Of Aristotle there is only the 'Αθηναίων Πολιτεία, the *Posterior Analytics*, and the Προτρεπτικός; nothing of the *Ethics*, the *Politics*, the *Rhetoric*, or the *Metaphysics*, or of the collections on natural history. In view of the difficulty of both these authors, it is perhaps not surprising that they did not form part of the curriculum of a small provincial community; but it is remarkable that Herodotus, who is both easy and attractive, and has a special interest for Egyptian readers, should be represented only by 10 examples. Other authors of whom there is some substantial representation are Aeschines (8), Apollonius Rhodius (8), Callimachus (9 and 2 commentaries), Hippocrates (6), and Theocritus (6).

On the whole, when it is remembered that these papyri come mainly from the rubbish heaps of small provincial towns, the range of literature represented must be regarded as fairly substantial. It shows that Greek literature was widely current among the ordinary Graeco-Roman population; that it held a prominent place in education, and that there was a reading public of considerable size. It can have no relation to the extent of literature that was available in a great literary centre such as Alexandria, Antioch, Athens, or the other important towns of the Greek world. Of this a better idea may be obtained from the collections of Athenaeus or Stobaeus, and the numerous quotations scattered about in other Greek authors. The papyrus discoveries dispose, however, of the suggestion that such compilations were derived mainly from anthologies; for if so much literature existed in the small towns and villages of Egypt, there is no ground for questioning the much wider comprehensiveness of the great libraries, to which scholars had access.

The distribution of the papyri in time is also instructive. It will be understood that conclusions on this head are necessarily precarious, partly because of the element of chance that attends the discoveries of papyri, and partly because datings of manuscripts can seldom be exact. Palaeographers differ in their opinions as to date, and often can venture only on approximate dates, such as 'ist–2nd century'. Still, the range of variation between experienced palaeographers is not very great; and if the manuscripts to which double dates are assigned are divided equally between the centuries given as alternatives, the results (as taken from Oldfather's list, which again depends on the original publications) are as follows:

3rd cent. B.C.	68 (including one of the late 4th)
2nd cent.	42
1st cent.	49
1st cent. A.D.	117
2nd cent.	341
3rd cent.	304
4th cent.	83
5th cent.	78
6th cent.	29
7th cent.	13

Only approximate as these figures may be, the main results stand out unmistakably. They show that the period of greatest dissemination of reading was in the second and third centuries of our era. This is the period when the Graeco-Roman occupation of Egypt was at its height. During the

Ptolemaic period the infiltration of a Greek population, and the assimilation of Greek culture by
the natives, were steadily growing. (The higher
figures for the third century B.C., as compared
with those for the second and first, may be accounted for by the larger discoveries of papyri of
that century, especially in the form of mummy
cartonnage.) After the Roman conquest, the
Graeco-Roman population, which was mainly
Greek-reading, greatly increased; and the first
three centuries of the Empire mark the climax of
Graeco-Roman culture in Egypt. The drop that
takes place in the fourth century is very marked,
and is to be accounted for partly by the general
decline of Roman civilization, and partly by the
spread of Christianity, which diverted attention
from pagan literature. From this decline there
was no recovery, until the Arab conquest in the
seventh century extinguished Christian and pagan
literature at once.

These figures of course relate only to Egypt, but
there is no reason to doubt their general applica-
bility to the Hellenistic world. The causes which
operated in Egypt operated also in Syria and Asia
Minor, and may be assumed to have produced
similar results. We are entitled therefore to draw
general conclusions as to the dissemination of
books and the practice of reading in the Hellenistic
world. During the last three centuries before

Christ, Greek literature was spreading over the
wide regions administered by the successors of
Alexander. The main centres, notably Alexandria,
but also Antioch, Pergamum, and the other great
cities of the Near East, were the seats of libraries
and the homes of scholars; and Greek literature
was the natural heritage of the Greek-speaking
population throughout the Hellenistic kingdoms.
There was a large output of literature, much of it
in the shape of commentaries and collections, a
good deal of it scientific and medical. There was
also a general habit of reading the great works of
previous ages, especially Homer, and after him
Demosthenes, Plato, Euripides, and Menander.
During the first three centuries of the Roman
Empire the same habits continued; then, with the
spread and official recognition of Christianity,
came an abrupt decline of humanistic culture.
Christian literature increases, but pagan literature
declines, until both alike are submerged in the
rising flood of Mohammedanism.

II

THE PAPYRUS ROLL

IN the previous chapter some account has been
given of the use of books and the practice of
reading in the Greek world, from the origins of
Greek literature down to the time when the spread
of Christianity begins seriously to affect the predominance of pagan literature, and Hellenism
passes into Byzantinism. So far, little has been
said of the material character and appearance of
the books in which Greek literature was preserved.
This is not a matter of merely antiquarian interest.
The external form of books has at all times affected
and been affected by their contents. The materials
available for writing have facilitated or impeded
the output of literature. Fashion and convenience
have dictated the size and shape of books, and
thereby have affected the scale and character of
their contents. Authors have planned their works
to suit the prevalent scale of books, or, on the other
hand, the scale of books has been altered to meet
the demand for a particular content. As will be
shown later, the demand for volumes containing
the whole of the accepted Christian scriptures had
much to do with the adoption of the vellum codex
as the predominant form of book from the fourth
century onwards. Similarly in the thirteenth
century the growth of education and of interest

in the Scriptures led to the production of small Bibles suitable for private use and convenient handling. Modern examples have been the prevalence of periodical publication, and subsequently of the three-volume novel, in the early Victorian age, and the change in the scale of novels caused by the demand for shorter and handier volumes.

It is therefore of importance to know, as fully as the extant evidence permits, the form of book which was prevalent in the ancient Greek world, and its bearing on the manner in which the literature of Greece was produced and circulated. It also has a bearing on textual criticism, since the restoration of corrupt passages is to some extent conditioned by the habits of ancient scribes. No excuse therefore seems to be required for setting out, even in somewhat minute detail, the present state of our knowledge with regard to the material of Greek books and the habitual practices of their transcribers. The details so supplied from our increased acquaintance with actual specimens of ancient books may serve literary criticism in the same way as the minute study of Jacobean printed books and manuscripts has recently served the criticism of Jacobean literature.

The period to be dealt with in this study of the ancient Greek book is approximately twelve hundred years, and for our present purpose it falls into two equal parts. For the first six hundred years we have no direct evidence (that is, no actual examples of books), and we are dependent upon rather scanty allusions and the consideration of probabilities. For the second six hundred years, not only is the indirect evidence more plentiful, in the shape of literary references and descriptions, but we have now, thanks to the discoveries of the last fifty years, a very considerable supply of actual specimens of books produced throughout the period.

It is necessary to begin with the material. The substances used for the reception of writing in the ancient world were numerous. Besides stone, which has always been a principal material for inscriptions, but which hardly comes within the category of book-production, the following may be mentioned. We have references to writing upon leaves, which have been much used in India and the adjoining countries down even to the present day. Bark has also been used in various parts of the world, and its early use in Italy seems to be proved by its having provided the Latin word for 'book'. Linen, according to Livy and the earlier chroniclers whom he followed, was the substance on which the ancient records and sacred books of Rome were written. Metals, such as gold (for amulets), bronze, iron, and especially lead, were employed to receive writing, though not, so far as we know, for writings on any extensive scale. Wood was much used for tablets, whether plain

or whitened or covered with wax, and many
specimens of them exist; more will have to be said
of them later. Potsherds were extensively used in
Egypt for accounts, schoolboy exercises, letters, and
short literary drafts. Far more important than all
these is clay, which was the universal material
for writing, whether of documents or of literary
works, in Mesopotamia, and was also used in the
Hittite Empire, in Syria, and in Crete. Hundreds
of thousands of such clay tablets have been brought
to light in the excavations of the last century.

None of these, however, come seriously into
consideration in connexion with Greek literature,
or with Roman literature of the classical period.
Wooden tablets were, no doubt, extensively used
for letters and note-books, and the earliest reference to writing in Greek literature, Homer's mention of the message carried by Bellerophon, is
plainly to such a tablet; but this is not book-
production in the ordinary sense of the term.
Specimens of writing on metals also exist, but these
are mainly either amulets or imprecations, or the
certificates of discharge given to retired Roman
soldiers. The only reference to use of a more
literary kind is the statement of Pausanias that the
Boeotians of Helicon showed him a sheet of lead
(μόλυβδος), much decayed, on which was inscribed
the *Works and Days*.[1] Obviously much more than

[1] Pausanias, ix. 31, 4.

a single sheet would have been required for the whole poem; but in any case this would be an exceptional production.

There remain three materials of which more must be said, and of which two are of prime importance. These are leather, papyrus, and vellum. Leather has been, at various times and in various places, somewhat extensively used as a vehicle for writing. In Egypt there is mention of documents written on skins in the time of the Fourth Dynasty, and actual specimens are extant from about 2000 b.c. On Assyrian monuments scribes are shown holding rolls which appear to be of leather; but neither in Egypt nor in Mesopotamia was this material ever in general use. In Persia, however, it appears to have been used, if Ctesias's reference to the βασιλικαὶ διφθέραι from which he professes to derive his knowledge of early Persian history is to be trusted. Coming nearer to the Greek world we have the statement of Herodotus (v. 58) that the Ionians had from antiquity called books διφθέραι, because once, when papyrus was scarce, they had made use of goatskins and sheepskins. He adds that even in his own time many barbarous peoples used skins as writing materials. No doubt he would have included under this head the peoples of Syria and Palestine, where we know leather to have been regularly used. The Talmud requires all copies of the Law to be written on skins, and in roll form; and many examples of such rolls are in existence. In this the Talmudists were no doubt only confirming the existing and traditional practice; and such evidence as exists tends to support this view. The copies of the Hebrew Scriptures which were taken to Egypt in the third century B.C., for the purposes of the Septuagint translation, are expressly said to have been written on διφθέραι.[1] The statement in Jer. xxxvi. 23 that Jehoiakim used the scribe's scraping-knife (τῷ ξυρῷ τοῦ γραμματέως) to destroy the roll of Jeremiah's prophecies implies that they were written on a material stronger than papyrus. A knife was (as in the Middle Ages) part of a scribe's equipment for making corrections on leather or vellum, just as a sponge was for the writer on papyrus.

We cannot therefore exclude the possibility that works of Greek literature may sometimes have been written on leather; but we have no direct evidence of it, and in any case the practice can only be supposed to have existed in very early times.[2] All the evidence goes to show that the one material in

---

[1] 'Letter of Aristeas', ed. Thackeray in Swete's *Introduction to the Old Testament in Greek*, pp. 519, 549.

[2] The reference to skins in a fragment of Euripides (fr. 629, Nauck, quoted by Gardthausen)—

εἰσὶν γάρ, εἰσὶ διφθέραι μελαγγραφεῖς
πολλῶν γέμουσαι Λοξίου γηρυμάτων

cannot be taken to rest on real archaeological knowledge, but is intended to suggest great antiquity, and implies a tradition to this effect.

general use in the Greek lands at least from the
sixth century B.C. onwards was papyrus. The passage just quoted from Herodotus shows that he,
writing in the middle of the fifth century, could
not conceive of a civilized people using any
material other than papyrus, except under the
pressure of necessity. All the copies of earlier
Greek authors known to him must therefore have
been written on papyrus, and these may be presumed to have extended back for at least two or
three generations before his time. We are therefore justified in taking it as certain that the use of
papyrus covers at least the period of the lyric poets,
and there is no reason why it should not be carried
back even to the beginnings of Greek literature.
We know that papyrus was used in Egypt as far
back as the third millennium, if not earlier; and
there is no other material, with the possible exception of leather, which would have been easily
available for the Greeks. If, therefore, there was
writing (as I have endeavoured to prove) in the
days of Homer, it is a probable corollary that the
material used was papyrus; and quite certainly
it was the material in principal use during the
great days of Attic literature and throughout the
Hellenistic period.[1]

[1] The assertion of Varro, quoted by Pliny (*Nat. Hist.* xiii. 11),
that the use of papyrus as a material for books was only discovered
after Alexandria's conquest of Egypt and the foundation of
Alexandria is negligible, for we have large numbers of Egyptian

In describing, therefore, the papyrus book we are describing the main vehicle of literature in the classical world; and for this we have ample evidence, both from literary allusions and from the existence of actual specimens.

Papyrus,[1] the writing material, was manufactured out of the pith of a water-plant, *Cyperus papyrus,* which in antiquity grew plentifully in the waters of the Nile. It was not unknown in other parts of the ancient world, but Egypt, and particularly the Delta, was the main place of its cultivation. To-day it survives only in the upper reaches of the Nile, far beyond the frontiers of Egypt, and sporadically also in Sicily and Syria. Theophrastus[2] and Pliny[3] describe it as a plant growing in 6 feet of water or less, with a total height of as much as 15 feet, and a stem as thick as a man's wrist. Different parts of it were used for different purposes—for fuel, for boats, for ropes, for sails; but the use that has given it a world-wide reputation is that of its pith for the manufacture of writing material.

books written on papyrus from about 2000 B.C. downwards, and the statement is inconsistent with the references in Herodotus and elsewhere. Pliny himself did not believe it, remarking shortly afterwards (c. 13), 'ingentia quidem exempla contra Varronis sententiam de chartis reperiuntur'.

[1] In the following pages I have freely used two earlier articles of my own, 'The Papyrus Book' (*The Library*, 1926), and *Ancient Books and Modern Discoveries* (Caxton Club, Chicago, 1927).

[2] *Hist. Plant.* iv. 8. 3.   [3] *Nat. Hist.* xiii. 11.

The supply of papyrus appears to have been a government monopoly in Egypt, and to have been farmed out to individual undertakers. Among the Tebtunis papyri is a document of the second century (No. 308) containing a receipt for 20,000 papyrus stems, bought from two μισθωταὶ δρυμῶν καὶ ἐρήμου αἰγιαλοῦ Πολέμωνος μερίδος.

The *locus classicus* on its manufacture is Pliny, *Nat. Hist.* xiii. 11, 12.[1] The unit of manufacture was the single sheet (κόλλημα). The pith having been cut with a sharp knife into thin strips, these strips were laid down in two layers, in one of which the fibres were placed horizontally, in the other vertically. The two layers were then fastened together by moisture, glue, and pressure until they formed one fabric—a fabric which, though now so brittle that it can easily be crumpled into dust, probably had a strength nearly equal to that of good paper. This is shown by the fact that pumice-stone, in addition to a mallet and ivory or shell polishers, was used to give it a smooth surface. The central portion of the pith was best, and was therefore used for the highest class of writing material; the portions nearer the rind were employed only for inferior qualities. The size of the sheets in which the material was manufactured differed according to the length in which the strips could be cut without weakness or fracture. The

[1] See Appendix.

best quality was that in which the horizontal strips were longest; and our ancient authorities and measurements from existing specimens concur to prove that, although specimens exist of sheets as wide as 15 inches, yet normally about 9 inches was the width of a sheet of the best papyrus, while those of more ordinary quality might measure 6 or 5 inches or even less. In the Roman market different qualities of papyrus, with their different sizes, were known by different names (Claudia, Augusta, Livia, hieratica, amphitheatrica, Fanniana, Saïtica, Taeniotica, emporetica, in descending order of merit), but this statement of Pliny represents only Roman practice. There is nothing to show that the same classification existed in Egypt, and it is impossible to identify the several categories in the papyri that have actually been found.

All that can be said is that in the best papyri, in which the quality of the material is obviously superior, the width of the sheets of which the roll is composed is usually greater. A few examples may be given from papyri in the British Museum. Several of the best Egyptian papyri have sheets of as much as 10½ inches in width, and in some they exceed 12 inches. In the Papyrus of Nu the sheets actually reach a width of 15 inches. The Ani Papyrus, probably the finest extant Egyptian book, has sheets of 12–13 inches. The Hunefer Papyrus has sheets varying between 10 and 11½ inches. In the Greenfield Papyrus, on the other hand, which is a finely written hieratic roll, they are not more than 8¼ inches. The height of Egyptian papyri is often very great. The Greenfield Papyrus measures 19 inches in height; the Harris Papyrus I is 17 inches, the Ani Papyrus 15 inches, and the Papyri of Nu and Nekht 13½ inches.

For Greek papyrus rolls the measurements are conspicuously smaller. Probably the finest Greek literary papyrus is a copy of Book III of the *Odyssey* (Brit. Mus. pap. 271). This is composed of κολλή-ματα measuring 13 ×9 inches. A fine manuscript at Berlin, containing a commentary on Plato's *Theae-tetus*, has sheets measuring 12½ ×10 inches. In the Bacchylides Papyrus, also a fine manuscript, they measure 9¾×8 or 9 inches; in the principal Hyperides MS. (B.M. papp. 108 + 115), 12 ×10 inches. Other examples are as follows:

B.M. pap. 132, Isocrates, *De Pace*, 11×7¾ to 8¾ in.
Bodl. Gr. class. A. 1 (P), *Iliad*, ii, 10⅞× 10½ in.
B.M. pap. 742, *Iliad*, ii, 10¾×8½ in. (about).
B.M. pap. 128, *Iliad*, xxiii, xxiv, 9¾× 5 to 6 in.
B.M. pap. 134, Hyperides, *In Philippidem*, 9¼×7½ in.

Other papyri of exceptional height are B.M. pap. 736 (*Il.* viii), which is 12½ inches high; P. Oxy. 843 (Plato, *Symposium*) and 844 (Isocrates, *Pane-gyricus*), both 12¼ inches; P. Oxy. 448 (*Od.* xxii, xxiii), 11¾ inches; and P. Tebt. 265 (*Il.* ii), 11½ inches; but the width of the κολλήματα of these is either unascertainable or unrecorded. P. Tebt. 268 (Dictys Cretensis) surpasses all these in height, measuring 13 inches; but it is written on the back of a non-literary document, and these not infrequently exceeded the height measurements of literary manuscripts. The tallest Greek papyrus known to me (B.M. pap. 268) is a tax-register, measuring 15½ inches in height; but the κολλήματα are only 5 inches wide. It may be added that two very carefully written petitions (B.M. papp. 354 and 177), for which no doubt papyrus of good quality was selected, are written on single sheets measuring 8½ and 6¼ inches in width respectively.

It may be taken, therefore, as established by experience that a papyrus sheet intended for a roll on which a work of Greek literature might be inscribed rarely, if ever, exceeded 13 ×9 inches, while something like 10 ×7½ would be more common for a book of moderate pretensions. On the other hand, pocket volumes of poetry might be of much less height. The papyrus containing the Mimes of Herodas is about 5 inches high, and a Hibeh papyrus of the third century B.C., containing a comedy, is almost the same. The smallest papyrus roll known is one at Berlin (Pap. 10571, *Berliner Klassikertexte*, v. 1, 75), containing epigrams, which is less than 2 inches high.

Our papyrus manufacturer has thus produced his material in sheets of his selected size. Such sheets could be used singly for letters or short documents (the second and third Epistles of St. John would have gone on such single sheets), but for literary purposes they were not thus sold separately. On the contrary a number of sheets (a phrase of Pliny, *numquam plures scapo quam vicenae*, appears to give twenty as an extreme limit) were glued together, side by side, to form a continuous roll, and in this form the material was placed on the market. Of course the author was not limited by the length of the unit in which he bought his material. If his work did not extend to the length of a roll of twenty sheets, he could cut off the superfluous material. If it was of greater length, he could glue on a second roll to the first. Pliny's phrase has been misunderstood to mean that no roll, when produced as a completed book, ever exceeded the length of twenty sheets; but this is absurd in itself (since it would imply rolls of not more than 15 feet length at the maximum), and is disproved by facts.[1]

The length of a roll, when inscribed and issued for circulation as a work of literature, was no doubt a matter of convenience and custom; and for our present purpose this is a fact of vital

[1] Egyptian rolls exist on which the number 20 is marked at the end of each twentieth κόλλημα, no doubt indicating the end of each length of papyrus as purchased by the author from his stationer (Borchardt, *Zeitschr. fur ägyptische Sprache*, xxvii. 120; Wilcken, *Hermes*, xxviii. 167).

importance. We can judge the prevalent fashion from the evidence of papyrus rolls that have survived. Here we find a marked difference between ancient Egyptian and Greek practice. Egyptian rolls sometimes exceed 100 feet in length, and often exceed 50; here are a few examples:

Harris Papyrus I (B.M. 9999), 133 ft. × 17 in.
Greenfield Papyrus (B.M. 10554), 123 ft. × 19 in.
Papyrus of Nebseni (B.M. 9900), 77 ft. × 8¾ in.
Papyrus of Ani (B.M. 10470), 76 ft. × 15 in.
Papyrus of Nu (B.M. 10477), 65½ ft. × 13½ in.
Papyrus of Nekht (B.M. 10471), 46½ ft. × 13½ in.

It is true that nearly all of these are ceremonial copies of the Book of the Dead, not meant to be read, but to be buried in the tomb of a rich owner, and that literary texts are usually on much shorter rolls; but the longest of all, the Harris Papyrus of 133 feet, is a panegyrical chronicle of the reign of Rameses II.

For Greek papyri the figures are very different. Here are some examples, taken either from direct measurement of such few complete rolls as exist, or, more often, by calculation in the case of fragmentary copies of known works:

P. Grenf. 4 (*Il.* xxii–xxiv), 35 ft.
P. Oxy. 224 (Euripides, *Phoenissae*), 34 ft.
B.M. 108 + 115 (Hyperides, three orations, incomplete), 28 ft.
P. Oxy. 26 (Demosthenes, Προοίμια), c. 28 ft.

P. Oxy. 27 (Isocrates, Περὶ 'Αντιδόσεως), 25 ft.
P. Oxy. 843 (Plato, *Symposium*), 23½ ft.
P. Oxy. 844 (Isocrates, *Panegyricus*), 23⅓ ft.
P. Oxy. 16 (Thucydides, Bk. iv), 23 ft.
B.M. 128 (*Il.* xxiii, xxiv), 20 ft.
P. Tebt. 265 (*Il.* ii), *c.* 19 ft.
B.M. 132 (Isocrates, Περὶ Εἰρήνης), 14 ft.

The British Museum Odyssey papyrus, already
referred to as the handsomest specimen of Greek
book-production, would have required 7 feet if it
contained only Book III, or 21 feet if it originally
included Books I–III. The Bacchylides Papyrus
now measures about 15 feet, but we do not know
how much is missing; and the same is the case
with the papyrus of Herodas, of which the surviving portion measures 14½ feet, with a height of
only 5 inches.

The net result then would appear to be that
35 feet may be taken to be the extreme limit of
a normal Greek literary roll. The only two instances which seem to require a greater length are
P. Petrie 5 (3rd cent. B.C.) of Plato's *Phaedo* and
P. Oxy. 225 (1st cent.) of Thucydides, Book II,
which would each have occupied about 50 feet.
Either, therefore, the book in each of these cases
occupied two rolls, or they must be regarded as
exceptional. The general rule appears to be well
established on a wide basis of proof.

On the roll thus formed the writing was arranged

in a series of columns (σελίδες). It is clear that
the roll was made up before it was written on; the
scribe did not write his text on separate sheets and
then unite them to form a roll, for the writing
frequently runs over the junction of the sheets.
The κολλήματα (sheets of papyrus) are therefore
quite distinct from the σελίδες (columns of writing). In the case of poetical texts, the width of
the column is fixed by the length of the lines. Thus
in a papyrus of the second book of the *Iliad* at
Oxford (Bodl. Gr. class. A. 1 (P)), written in an
exceptionally large hand, the width of the column
of writing is about $7\frac{1}{2}$ inches, or $9\frac{3}{4}$ inches including the margin. A similar manuscript of the
same book in the British Museum (B.M. pap. 742
= P. Oxy. 20) has about the same measurements.
In the British Museum *Odyssey* the column is
about 5 inches wide, or $6\frac{1}{2}$ inches with the margin;
in the Bacchylides MS. they vary between 4 and
$5\frac{1}{2}$ inches, including margin. In the earliest
known literary papyrus, the MS. of Timotheus at
Berlin, they vary between $6\frac{1}{4}$ and 10 inches; but
this is an exceptional case, the writing being a large,
heavy uncial, which takes up a great deal of room.

In prose works, where the scribe was at liberty
to choose his own length of line, the measurements are much smaller. The following are some
examples, including margins, for which about
$\frac{1}{2}$ inch must be allowed in each case:

Louvre Hyperides, 4 in.

P. Oxy. 842 (Ephorus, *Hellenica*), 4 in.

P. Oxy. 843 (*Symposium*), 3½ in.

Berlin *Theaetetus* commentary, 3¼ in. (with exceptionally wide margin).

B.M. pap. 132 (Isocrates), 3¼ in.

P. Petrie 5 = B.M. pap. 688 (Plato's *Phaedo*), 3 in.

B.M. papp. 108+115 (Hyperides), 2¾ in. (margins rather wide).

B.M. pap. 133 (Demosthenes, *Epistles*), 3 in.

B.M. pap. 134 (Hyperides, *In Philippidem*), 2¼ in.

P. Oxy. 666 (Aristotle, Προτρεπτικός), 1¾ in.

In general it may be said that 3½ inches or more is exceptionally wide, 2 inches or less exceptionally narrow, for the actual column of writing. Between 2 and 3 inches is the normal width in a well-written papyrus.[1] The large British Museum Hyperides, which is a good specimen, has columns of about 2 inches of writing, with about ¾ inch of margin. Literary texts written in non-literary hands, such as the Ἀθηναίων Πολιτεία, where one column extends to as much as 11 inches of writing, cannot be taken as evidence of the normal methods of book production.[2]

[1] Of 38 manuscripts of which the dimensions are given by Milne (*Cat. of Literary Papyri in the British Museum*, 1927), 27 have columns of writing from 2 to 3 inches in width; in 5 they are less than 2 inches, in 6 they are more than 3 inches. Exceptional manuscripts, such as the Ἀθηναίων Πολιτεία, are not included.

[2] It is the use of narrow columns that seems to be the point in

The number of lines in a column, and the number of letters in a line of prose, naturally depend to some extent on the size of the writing. It will, however, be useful to give some figures, since textual critics not infrequently base calculations as to conjectural emendations on estimates of the probable content of a line or a column. The number of lines in a column of a given papyrus roll does not usually vary much, though it is seldom absolutely uniform. On the other hand there is often considerable variety in the number of letters in a line. Scribes made no effort (as was the practice in medieval vellum manuscripts) to enclose their column of text in a precise rectangle. The outer (right-hand) edge of the column was allowed to be ragged and irregular. There were strict rules as to the permissible divisions of words between two lines,[1] and the scribe would extend

a passage in Suetonius' *Caesar* (c. 56), to which my attention was drawn by Professor H. E. Butler:

'Epistolae quoque eius ad senatum extant, quas primus videtur ad paginas et formam memorialis libelli convertisse, cum antea consules et duces nonnisi transversa charta scriptas mitterent.'

Caesar's predecessors had contented themselves with writing their dispatches across the width of a sheet of papyrus, in one broad column. Caesar (writing probably at greater length) sent his in the form of a small roll, with columns of the narrow width usual in works of prose literature. The expression is obscure to us, though doubtless clear to Suetonius's contemporaries; but this seems the most probable explanation.

[1] These are stated in my *Palaeography of Greek Papyri* (p. 31).

or reduce the number of letters in a line in order to reach the end of a word or a permissible division. If the line was short, a small filling-mark ($<$) was often used. A few figures will serve to show characteristic lengths of columns and of lines, and the limits of variation:

	Lines in column.	Letters in line.[1]
Louvre Hyperides (2nd cent. B.C.)	26–28	30 (27–33)
B.M. Hyperides, *In Philippidem* (1st cent.)	26–28	17 (16–19)
B.M. Hyperides, *In Demosthenem*, &c. (1st cent. A.D.)	28 (27–30)	16 (13–18)
P. Oxy. 16 (Thucydides, 1st cent.)	49–52	19–23
B.M. 132 (Isocrates, late 1st cent.)	*c.* 45	20–24
P. Oxy. 844 (Isocrates, 2nd cent.)	39–41	18 (14–19)
P. Oxy. 843 (Plato, 2nd–3rd cent.)	*c.* 47	28 (23–32)
Chester Beatty Deuteronomy (2nd cent. codex)	31–38	16 (13–19)
Chester Beatty Daniel (3rd cent. codex)	45–46	18 (16–19)

These figures, which might be considerably extended, show that columns of less than 25 lines

---

[1] Figures outside brackets give the more usual number of lines or letters, those inside brackets the observed variations. The latter are not based on exhaustive examinations, so that even greater variations may exist.

TEACHER AND STUDENTS WITH ROLLS

are, to say the least, rare, and that lines with less than a normal 16 letters are equally so. The normal figures may be anything between 25 and 45 lines to a column,[1] and about 18 to 25 letters to a line. There are columns of exceptional height or smallness of writing which exceed these dimensions, but they are rare, and there may be a few manuscripts which fall below them; but even the Herodas papyrus, which is only 5 inches in height, and may be taken to represent a pocket volume of poetry, has 15–19 (usually 18) lines to a column. Hibeh Pap. 6 (a comedy), which is of the same height, has 23 lines to a column. It is also clear that conjectures which assume a fixed number of lines to a column, or of letters to a line, are not to be depended on when dealing with papyri.

The size of the margins, as in a modern book, varies with the pretensions of the book to beauty of appearance. In the large Hyperides MS. the upper margin is $2\frac{1}{2}$ inches, the lower 3 inches, with $\frac{3}{4}$ inch between the columns; in the Berlin *Theaetetus* commentary the measurements are respectively $1\frac{3}{4}$ inches, $2\frac{1}{2}$ inches, and 1 inch. It will be seen that the ancient book-designer realized the true proportions of margins much as a modern book-designer does, though the upper margin is

[1] Of 70 pagan manuscripts listed by Milne, of which these particulars are given, 47 have from 25 to 45 lines to a column; 12 have less, 11 have more. Only 3 have less than 20 (all poetry), and only 6 more than 50 (3 prose, 3 poetry).

perhaps rather larger in proportion to the lower than modern taste prefers. In the humbler class of books, as now, margins are much curtailed; and most of the papyri that have been discovered, which come from provincial Egypt, are of this kind. It is only the more handsomely written manuscripts (which would be the least likely to be disfigured by additions of this kind) that give much scope for those marginal notes and additions with which conjectural criticism sometimes makes such free play.[1]

At the beginning of a roll a space equivalent to about the width of a column seems often to have been left blank,[2] no doubt with the object of giving the reader something to hold the roll by when reading it, and also of protecting the text from injury through accidental tearing. This space was not utilized, as might have been expected, to receive the title of the work. Titles, when they appear at all, are appended at the end, as in early printed books.

Certain external additions have to be mentioned to complete the description of the papyrus book. We know from references in Latin literature that in books with any pretensions to style rollers were attached to the ends of the papyrus, and these

[1] Amherst Pap. ii. 13 has exceptionally wide margins between the columns, apparently for the reception of scholia.

[2] Examples are to be seen in the 'Aθηναίων Πολιτεία and Herodas papyri.

rollers were ornamented with projecting knobs (*cornua, umbilici*), which might be of various shapes or colours.[1] So far as I am aware, no examples of these have yet been found; so they must not be taken as characteristic of the cheaper class of books. In some cases, however, the ends of the

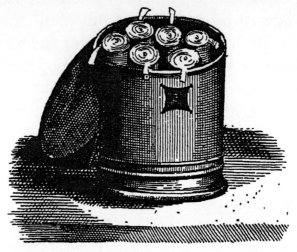

A book-box (*capsa*) containing rolls with sillybi. From *Antichità di Ercolano*.

roll are strengthened by an extra thickness of papyrus; and I have seen some burnt papyrus rolls which had quills attached to one end, to serve as rollers. In some cases the roll was provided with a wrapper of parchment (*membrana*), to protect it when not in use;[2] and these could be made ornamental by colouring. The purpose of lettering on

[1] Hence the phrases 'ad umbilicum pervenire' (Martial, iv. 91) or 'explicatum usque ad sua cornua librum' (Horace, *Epod.* xiv. 8).   [2] Tibullus, iii. 1. 9, Martial, iii. 2. 7.

the back of a modern book was served by project-ing—labels ($\sigma i \lambda \lambda \upsilon \beta o\iota$), of papyrus or vellum, on which the title of the book was inscribed. This hung outwards as the rolls lay on the shelves of bookcases (*scrinia*) or stood in the buckets (*capsae*) in which, as appears both from pictures and from literary references, they were often stored.[1] A few examples have survived.[2]

The writing on a papyrus roll was normally on one side only, and that the side on which the papyrus fibres ran horizontally (known as the *recto*). If the text was continued on the back (*verso*), the roll was described as *opisthograph*. These, so far as extant examples are concerned, are very rare. The principal example known to me is a large magical roll in the British Museum (B.M. pap. 121), but there are several references to such books in literature, generally with the implication either that they were due to economy or that they were not intended for publication. The younger Pliny, describing his uncle's prodigious activity, says that he left a hundred and sixty volumes of notes, written back and front in an extremely minute hand.[3] Lucian's Diogenes tells his disciple, as a symptom of the life of poverty which he will

---

[1] Ovid, *Tristia*, i. 1. 109–10.
[2] B.M. pap. 801 (= P. Oxy. 301), P. Oxy. 1091. P. Oxy. 957 is a leather strip, apparently used for a similar purpose on a roll of official documents.
[3] *Epp.* iii. 5.

have to lead, that his wallet will be full of books written back and front.[1] On the other hand, when Juvenal (i. 1. 5) describes a colossal poem as 'summi plena iam margine libri Scriptus et in tergo necdum finitus Orestes', or when Ezekiel sees in his vision (ii. 10) a roll of a book written within and without with lamentations and mourning and woe, the emphasis is rather on the excess of material than on the poverty of the writer. Usually when writing is found on the *verso* of a papyrus, it is to be understood that the writer, unable or unwilling to obtain new papyrus, had recourse to the back of a roll already used for another work. Such books were evidently either intended for private use, or, if for sale, represented the cheapest form of book-production. Notable examples are the ᾽Αθηναίων Πολιτεία of Aristotle, written on the back of a roll of farm accounts; the Funeral Oration of Hyperides, a schoolboy's copy on the back of an astrological treatise; the Oxyrhynchus historical work (P. Oxy. 842), on the back of a land-register; Pindar's *Paeans* (P. Oxy. 841), on the back of a list of names; and (a rare example of the use of the *verso* of a literary work) the Epistle to the Hebrews, on the back of an Epitome of Livy (B.M. 1532 = P. Oxy. 657, 668).

From the limits which usage prescribed for the length of a papyrus roll it follows that no work of

[1] *Vit. Auct.* 9.

any considerable extent could be contained on a
single roll. An idea of the amount which a roll
could contain may be given by saying that a roll
of about 32–35 feet would hold, in a medium-sized
hand, one of the longer books of the New Testament (Matthew, Luke, or Acts), or a book of
Thucydides, but no more.[1] The first four books
of Herodotus and the seventh are about 25 per
cent. or more longer; the other four are a little
shorter. The books of Plato's *Republic* and *Laws*
are considerably shorter; two of them would
occupy about the same space as one of Thucydides.
Two or three books of the *Iliad* were as much as
an ordinary roll could contain; a papyrus of 20
feet in the British Museum, of good average
quality, contains the last two books. P. Oxy. 448
might have contained the last six books of the
Odyssey without exceeding normal dimensions; but
this is written on the *verso* of the papyrus, so is not
an example of normal book-production. The division of a single book into two rolls was not, however, unknown; thus Pliny, in describing his uncle's
works, speaks of 'studiosi tres (libri), in sex volu-
mina propter amplitudinem divisi'—which, however, implies that such a practice was not usual.

Another consequence of the size of the roll is

---

[1] On a computation, the second book of Thucydides contains
almost exactly the same number of words as the Gospel of
St. Matthew (*sc.* about 18,000).

that collected editions of an author's work could
not exist, except in the sense that the rolls containing them could be kept in the same bucket, which
might bear the label *Homer* or *Thucydides* or *Plato*.[1]
Volumes containing the whole corpus of an author's
work only became possible after the invention of
the codex, and especially of the vellum codex.
Before that time, the popularity of one work did
not confer immortality on its less popular brethren,
and it was easy for the seven plays of Aeschylus or
Sophocles to survive, while the rest perished.

We are now in a position to form a picture of
a book as known to the Greeks and Romans during
the best period of their literature. When closed
and not in use it was a roll of light-coloured
material,[2] generally about 9 or 10 inches in height,
and forming a cylinder of about an inch or an
inch and a half in diameter. When opened, it
displayed a series of columns of about 3 inches
in width (or more if it was poetry), with margins
of about half an inch between the columns, and

[1] Cf. the Acts of the Scillitan martyrs (A.D. 180): 'Saturninus
proconsul dixit, Quae sunt res in capsa vestra? Speratus dixit,
Libri et epistolae Pauli viri iusti.' This seems to imply that the
books in question were rolls, not codices.

[2] The papyri as we know them to-day, when they have not
been exceptionally stained by substances with which they have
been in contact, are generally of a pale yellow or straw tint, but
were probably lighter when new. Tibullus even describes a book
as snow-white: 'Lutea sed niveum involvat membrana libellum'
(iii. 1. 9).

upper and lower margins varying according to
the sumptuousness of the book-production. Its
total length did not normally exceed 35 feet, and
the reader unfolded it with his right hand and

A reader holding a roll of papyrus. From *Antichità
di Ercolano*, vol. v, tav. 55.

rolled it up with his left as the reading proceeded.
When not in use it was placed in a bucket or lay
on a shelf in a cupboard, possibly wrapped in a
parchment cover, with its title visible on a projecting label. Large libraries, such as those of
Alexandria, might contain collections of hundreds
of thousands of such rolls; but in Greek times, at
any rate, large private libraries do not seem to

have been common. Small libraries, however, such such as might be contained in a single cupboard or a small room, may have been plentiful after the beginning of the Alexandrian period.

The lack of assistances to readers, or of aids to facilitate reference, in ancient books is very remarkable. The separation of words is practically unknown, except very rarely when an inverted comma or dot is used to mark a separation where some ambiguity might exist. Punctuation is often wholly absent, and is never full and systematic. The Bacchylides MS. is more fully supplied than usual. Where it exists at all, it is generally either in the form of a single dot (almost always above the level of the line), or of a blank space, often accompanied by a short stroke (παράγραφος) below the first letters of the line in which the pause in the sense occurs. In dramatic texts, such as the Petrie *Antiope* MS. or the Herodas, the παράγραφος is employed to indicate a change of speaker; but the name of the speaker is hardly ever given. In the Bacchylides MS. the παράγραφος marks the ends of strophes or epodes. Titles of works and authors' names, if given at all, are added at the end of the work, not at the beginning; but in the Bacchylides MS. a second hand has written them in the margin at the beginning of each ode, and in the Herodas the title of each mime is regularly written by the first hand at the beginning. The end of a work is sometimes marked by a rather elaborate flourish (*coronis*) in the margin. Accents are very rarely used; they are most plentiful in two early lyrical manuscripts, those of Bacchylides and Alcman. Breathings are still more rare, but a square rough breathing is occasionally added, especially with relative pronouns, where otherwise obscurity might be caused. Where accents or breathings do occur, they have, oftener than not, been added subsequently by a different hand.

Normally, therefore, it is clear that the reader was expected to be able to understand his text without any of the aids to which we are accustomed. It is extraordinary that so simple a device as the separation of words should never have become general until after the invention of printing; although, with a little practice, it is not so difficult to read an undivided text as might be supposed. It must also have been very difficult to find a given passage when required, and impossible to give a reference to it which could be generally applied. References can only be given to a particular book in a work long enough to be so divided; never to a page or line. How Aristotle or Pliny, for example, could find their way about their vast collections of materials is difficult to understand; and Homeric criticism must have been much impeded by the impossibility of referring to the line, as well as the book, of the required passage. Further, unless a roll were supplied with a σίλλυβος, it was necessary to unroll it to the end in order to ascertain the author and title. It cannot be denied that throughout the classical period the technique of book-production left something to be desired, and that the convenience of the reader was little consulted.

The agent by whom, throughout this period, books were produced was, of course, the individual scribe; and of him and his ways something may be said. The great contrast between the manuscript and the printed book is the contrast between individualism and mass production; and, so far as appears from the available evidence, this individualism was at its greatest in the classical period. In the Middle Ages the art of transcription was organized. Manuscripts were written in monastic scriptoria, each of which tended to develop its own characteristics, so that it is often possible to say, not merely that a given manuscript was produced in the twelfth or thirteenth century, but that it was the work of a particular scriptorium, of Tours or Corbie, of St. Albans or Bury St. Edmunds. In the classical world there is little evidence of such organization. During the pre-Alexandrian period there was small scope for it. Reading, as we have seen, was so little thought of, and the total number of books must have been so small, that there cannot have been much demand

for an organized corps of scribes. Even when the
output of books increased vastly, the evidence of
organization remains slight. We do indeed hear
of a great literary patron, such as Maecenas, having his own establishment of copyists; but such
references are scanty, and we do not know how
far, even in such establishments, uniformity of
practice was carried.

It is probable that the nearest approach to a
medieval scriptorium would have been found in
the Museum at Alexandria, where we know that
the Ptolemies made a practice of copying books
on a large scale, or in other large libraries such as
Pergamum. If we had the output of such libraries
before us, we might see there the evidence of the
formation of localized styles or schools of handwriting. But even this would go but a short way
towards a general stereotyping of style. It is quite
clear, from the evidence with which Egypt pro-
vides us, that a great amount of the total book-
production was of local and even private origin.
In the Middle Ages, at any rate until a late period,
book-production was confined to monasteries,
where types of writing were domiciled, so that one
recognizes the work of a school, not of an individual scribe; but in Graeco-Roman Egypt books
might be produced anywhere and by anybody.
Some of the papyri that have come down to us
are the workmanship of highly skilled scribes, and

are beautiful examples of book-production. Others are good journeyman work, such as we may suppose any considerable provincial centre to have been capable of turning out. Others again are plainly non-professional work, transcripts made by an individual reader for his own use or by a half-educated slave under his direction. Perhaps the extreme instance is the well-known papyrus of Aristotle's Ἀθηναίων Πολιτεία, written by four distinct hands, of which one may be supposed to be that of the student who caused its production, another (very like the first and yet with quite distinctive characteristics) perhaps that of a relative, while the other two would appear to have been very imperfectly educated underlings.

The result of these conditions is much less uniformity than is found in the Middle Ages. It is possible to distinguish different periods of handwriting, to distinguish with some certainty a Ptolemaic manuscript from one of the Roman period, or a Roman from a Byzantine, and even to assign a given script with fair confidence to a particular century; but within this framework there are great varieties of individual hands. One must never expect, when confronted with a newly-discovered papyrus, to be able to find its exact counterpart elsewhere. Just occasionally close resemblances may exist between two manuscripts (e.g. two copies of the second book of the *Iliad*, which have

been referred to above), but this is a rare exception. As a rule the palaeographer must judge from
a general sense of style rather than by finding close
parallels.

In these circumstances it naturally follows that
there are great variations in the quality of workmanship found among the extant papyri—which,
be it remembered, are samples of the private
libraries of provincial Graeco-Roman Egypt. The
best are well and correctly written, equal in this
respect to the finest vellum manuscripts of a later
period; the worst—especially some of the products
of the decadence in the fourth and later centuries—
are almost incredibly bad, so that it is difficult to
understand how any one could have read them
with intelligence. Between these two extremes
every gradation exists. From this one deduction
may be drawn which is of some importance for
textual criticism, namely that scribes are capable
of anything. Not all mistakes, by any means, can
be accounted for by palaeographical causes. Often
they are mere incalculable blunders of a wandering
eye, of inattention, or of misplaced invention. The
result is greatly to complicate the task of the textual
critic, making the true restoration of a corrupt
passage at once more difficult to divine and often
impossible to demonstrate.

It is probable that manuscripts produced in one
of the great centres of learning were systematically

corrected; but in the more individualistic productions of which alone we have specimens this is never the case. Occasionally a miswritten word is corrected immediately above it, or an omitted word is added in the margin. Words which it is desired to cancel are usually marked by a dot above each letter. Probably the most frequent single cause of error, apart from mere slips of the pen, is the omission of a line (or more lines than one), whether on account of homoioteleuton or homoioarcton or merely by the accidental straying of the copyist's eye. Where such omissions have been noted, the usual method of rectification is to affix a mark somewhat like an anchor (⚓) opposite the place where the omission occurs, and to insert the missing line or lines, with a similar mark, in the upper or lower margin of the roll. It cannot, however, be said that the examples of this in the extant papyri are numerous.

The general conclusion is that in the better-written manuscripts the standard of accuracy, though not immaculate, is high, but that in privately produced copies or in what appear to be the lower grades of the book-trade errors might be plentiful. In the main centres of scholarship a still higher standard of accuracy may reasonably be supposed; and it is through them that the line of textual tradition must be presumed to run. Provincially produced copies, and still more those which were merely private ventures, can have left little mark on the tradition. Greek scribes never attained the meticulous accuracy of the copyists of the Hebrew Scriptures; but one is entitled to believe in the general fidelity of the transmission of classical texts, though not by any means in its infallibility.

So far we have been speaking only of the papyrus roll, which was practically the only form of book in use in the Greek world until well into the Christian era. Other considerations come into play when we reach the invention of the codex form of book, and again when vellum appears as the rival of papyrus. But before dealing with these, it will be well to say something of the use of books among the Romans, which overlaps that of the Greeks in the latter part of the period with which we are dealing.

III

BOOKS AND READING AT ROME

THE origins of writing in Italy are very obscure. In the Terramare and Villanova civilizations of the Bronze Age, preceding the foundation of Rome, there are no traces of writing. The Etruscans, who appear to have entered Italy early in the first millennium B.C., had or acquired the art of writing; but their extant inscriptions are of much later date, and as they are still undeciphered they give us little information. For the Romans themselves our information only begins with the chroniclers and antiquarians quoted by Livy and other writers; and they are themselves no earlier than the late third or second century. Their statements are often definite, but their authorities are unknown. There may be an element of tradition; more certainly there is an element of guessing and assumption. In reconstructing, therefore, the history of books in the earlier periods of Rome, we are building on very insecure foundations.[1]

For what they are worth, the following are the

---

[1] Livy's explanation of the obscurity of early Roman history is 'tum quod parvae et rarae per eadem tempora litterae fuere, una custodia fidelis memoriae rerum gestarum, et quod, etiam si quae in commentariis pontificum aliisque publicis privatisque erant monimentis, incensa urbe pleraeque interiere' (vi. 1).

statements made. Pliny[1] records a story told by
the annalist Cassius Hemina (writing in the first
half of the second century B.C.) of the discovery in
the consulship of P. Cornelius Cethegus and M.
Baebius Pamphilus (= 181 B.C.), by a scribe named
Cn. Terentius in a field on the Janiculum, of the
coffin of Numa, in which were books, written on
papyrus. Their preservation from damp and in-
sects is attributed to their having been enclosed in
a stone box, and anointed with cedar oil. Livy
also has a number of references to the use of writing
from the time of Numa onwards. Numa is said
to have appointed a high priest, to whom he entrusted written directions for the performance of
religious ceremonies.[2] Tullus Hostilius is said to
have found instructions with regard to certain
sacrifices among the memoirs (*commentarii*) of
Numa; and Ancus Martius ordered all the regula-
tions of Numa to be inscribed in a book (*album*)
and made public.[3] More solid, perhaps, are the
references to the Servian census.[4] If such a census
was made, as Roman tradition strongly believed,
it implies the use of writing; and the custom of a
census certainly appears to go back to an early
date. Not much stress can be laid on Livy's
reference to letters passing between the Tarquins
and their adherents in Rome, or to the presence

---

[1] *Nat. Hist.* xiii. 13.   [2] Livy, i. 20.
[3] Ibid. i. 31, 32.   [4] Ibid. i. 42, cf. iii. 3.

ROMAN INKPOTS

of a scribe in attendance on Lars Porsenna, whom
C. Mucius killed by mistake for the king. The
most one can say is that there may have been
some foundation for the very detailed narrative
which Livy was able to construct from his authorities,
such as Fabius Pictor, Licinius Macer, and others.
Since, however, he calls the former 'scriptorum
antiquissimus', it is implied that he knew no
historical writers earlier than the third century.
The story of the Sibylline books belongs to the
same period. From the fifth century we have the
story of a mission being sent to Athens to tran-
scribe the laws of Solon, and the tale of Virginius
includes a reference to the existence of schools
(*litterarum ludi*) in the Forum.

Frequent reference is made, generally on the
authority of Licinius Macer, who wrote in the
second century B.C., to the *libri lintei*, or books
written on linen, which were preserved in the
temple of Moneta. These appear to have been
registers of the names of magistrates.[1] Linen is

[1] 'His consulibus cum Ardeatibus foedus renovatum est; idque
monimenti est consules eos illo anno fuisse, qui neque in annalibus
priscis neque in libris magistratuum inveniuntur. . . . Licinius
Macer auctor est et in foedere Ardeatino et in linteis libris ad
Monetae ea inventa' (Livy, iv. 7). 'Nihil constat, nisi in libros
linteos utroque anno relatum inter magistratus praefecti nomen'
(ibid. c. 13). 'Qui si ea in re sit error, quod tam veteres annales, quod-
que magistratuum libri, quos linteos in aede repositos Monetae
Macer Licinius citat identidem auctores . . . habeant' (ibid. c. 20).
'Et Tubero et Macer libros linteos auctores profitentur' (ibid. c. 23).

elsewhere mentioned as a material for writing,[1] and an actual example exists in the principal relic of Etruscan writing, a long inscription or record found on the wrappings of a mummy of the late Greek or Roman period, and now in the museum at Agram. The date and extent, however, of the Roman *libri lintei* are unknown, and they appear to have perished before the time of Livy, since he does not claim to have seen them himself.[2]

Whatever may be the case, however, with regard to the existence of some form of written annals or lists of magistrates, it is quite clear that there was no Latin literature before the third century B.C., and that it then came into existence as a result of the introduction of Greek influences into Italy. The recognized father of Latin literature was Livius Andronicus; but he was in fact a Greek, who came to Rome in 272 B.C. and earned his living as a schoolmaster, for which purpose he translated the universal Greek school-book, Homer, into Latin, and also wrote the first Latin plays, based upon Greek originals. So also the first history of Rome, written about 200 B.C. by that Fabius Pictor to whom Livy refers as 'scriptorum

---

[1] e.g. Pliny, *Nat. Hist.* xiii. 11: 'postea publica monimenta plumbeis voluminibus, mox et privata linteis confici coepta.'

[2] Yet Vopiscus, in his life of Aurelian, says that the praefect of the city had promised him that even the *libri lintei* should be taken out of the Ulpian library (in the Forum of Trajan) for his use. But he does not say that he did in fact see them.

antiquissimus', was written in Greek. The earliest native Roman literature is represented by the verse *Annals* of Naevius (about 200 B.C.) and of Ennius (about 173 B.C.), and the *Origines* of Cato (about 160 B.C.). Thus it is not until the third century B.C., the period of the great Punic wars, that we can think of either books or readers as existing at Rome at all, and not until the century following that we can regard them as securely established.

With these authors, however, we do find the beginnings of a literature which, however indebted to Greek models, was Latin in language and Roman in character. In Naevius, Ennius, and Plautus we have substantial representatives of Latin epic and dramatic poetry, which imply the existence of a reading public and the circulation of books in manuscript. During the long crisis of the Second Punic War a literary society had little chance to establish itself; but in the next generation such a society was definitely formed, with the younger Scipio Africanus as its centre and patron, and Lucilius and Terence as its principal ornaments. Outside that circle, throughout the greater part of the century, and upholding Roman traditions against the overwhelming tide of Hellenism, there is the rugged figure of Cato, with his speeches, his miscellany of antiquarianism (the *Origines*), and his treatises on agriculture and a variety of other subjects. But Cato's nationalism was the hopeless effort of a die-hard. In spite of it, during the second century, Roman intellectual development became thoroughly hellenized. Roman authority, carrying with it Roman magistrates, soldiers, and agents of commerce, spread more and more to the east; Greek slaves were brought in increasing numbers to Rome; education was based upon Greek teaching and Greek text-books; the cultivated classes took to Greek literature as eagerly as the Italians of the Renaissance, and with far less difficulty; and Roman literature grew up upon Greek models, and formed its own metres on the basis of those of Greece.

It is not to be supposed that the habit of reading had yet spread very deeply among the mass of the population. Reading can go no farther than education takes it; and education was practically confined, as it was until quite recently in modern states, to a very limited class. Within that class, from the times of Scipio onward, we must suppose that books circulated freely, though the numbers of copies of any particular work need not have been great. Literature was studied for its own sake. Not only was the great Greek literature familiar to educated Romans, but the poems of Naevius and Ennius continued to be read and venerated by subsequent generations. With the Greek literature came Greek books, and Rome became familiar with the papyrus roll, which thenceforth was the standard form of book in the Latin, as it had long been in the Greek, world.

In the first century literature was fully domiciled in Rome. Cicero was perhaps by nature even more a man of letters than an orator or a politician. It is clear that he must have possessed a considerable library; and from this point we have no longer to consider the struggles of an originally exotic literature to establish itself. We can return to our proper subject, the use of books and the nature of the books used in the Roman world.

The poems of Catullus contain our earliest descriptions of the appearance of books, and Lucullus is particularly mentioned as the owner of a library—perhaps the first important private library in Rome. Lucullus is said not only to have collected large numbers of books, but to have thrown his library open freely to all who desired to use it, especially to the Greeks, who flocked thither as to a temple of the Muses.[1] Caesar also, according to Suetonius, commissioned Varro to collect books for a library which he proposed to found on a large scale.[2]

With the reign of Augustus the foundation of libraries became common. The first public library

---

[1] Suetonius, *Vit. Luculli*, c. 42.
[2] On the Roman libraries in general see J. W. Clark, *The Care of Books*, pp. 12–24.

(since that of Caesar never came into being) is said to have been founded by L. Asinius Pollio, the friend of Virgil and Horace; but shortly afterwards Augustus himself founded two libraries, one in the Campus Martius and one on the Palatine hill. Both were planned in the same way—a large open rectangular colonnade, within which stood a temple (or two temples in the case of the Porticus Octaviae in the Campus Martius) and two libraries, with a hall and perhaps other rooms. The two libraries were respectively for Greek and Latin books, in accordance with the plan designed by Caesar; and this example was followed by his successors. Incidentally this shows that the extant bulk of Latin literature was already able in some measure to maintain itself on an equality with that of Greece. The foundation of libraries became henceforth an imperial habit. Tiberius, Vespasian, and Trajan all built libraries at Rome, and Hadrian at Athens. The usual custom was to associate them with temples.

By the middle of the first century of our era, not only public but private libraries had become numerous, so much so that Seneca vehemently denounces the ostentatious accumulation of books. Books, he says, were accumulated not for learning but for show. The owner gathers thousands of books which he never reads, taking pleasure only in their ornamented ends (*frontes*) and their labels.

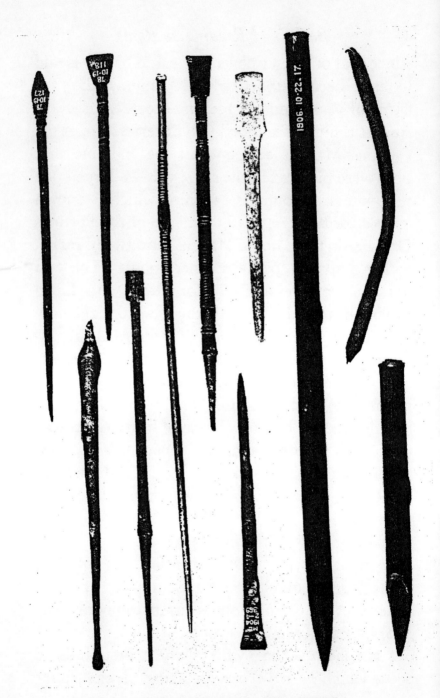

ROMAN PENS AND STYLI

The idlest of men own collections of all the orators and historians, stored in bookcases built up to the ceiling. A library is considered as essential an adornment of a house as a bathroom.[1] It is a little hard to understand how rows of rolls, lying upon shelves, could have been made effective as ornamentation; but it is to be remembered that the rolls themselves, or their covers, were stained with various colours, that they were adorned with projecting knobs of fine wood or ivory, and that the bookcases could be handsome pieces of furniture, often surmounted by busts or pictures of great authors.

A notable example of a private library is the only one which has actually been discovered with the books remaining on the shelves. This is the celebrated library found among the ruins of a villa at Herculaneum, which was overwhelmed by the great eruption of Vesuvius in A.D. 79. When this was excavated in 1754, a small room was found, about 12 feet square, in which were hundreds of rolls of papyrus, charred almost to cinders, among the remains of bookcases ornamented with inlaid woods. The bookcases had stood round the walls, and in the centre of the room was a table at which the books could be consulted. Nearly all of them are works of philosophy, especially Epicurean philosophy; and since many of them contain the writing

[1] Seneca, *De Tranquillitate Animi*, c. ix.

M

of Philodemus, a minor philosopher of the first
century B.C., and sometimes in two or more copies
of the same work, which no one except the author
would be likely to want, it has been concluded
that the villa is that of Philodemus himself or of
his patron, Piso. On palaeographical grounds the
papyri may be assigned to that date. They have
been partially unrolled and deciphered, though
with great difficulty, and they have a special
interest as the only considerable number of papyri
extant that were produced elsewhere than in
Egypt. It is only to be regretted that the owner
was not a collector of works of poetry or history,
instead of a philosopher. .

From the poets of the Imperial age, notably
Martial and Tibullus, we get many references to
the appearance of the books of their period. They
describe rolls of papyrus smoothed with pumice
and anointed with cedar-oil, with projecting knobs
of ivory or ebony, wrapped in purple covers, with
scarlet strings and labels. We are told of the booksellers' shops in the Argiletum, and of booksellers
such as Tryphon and Atrectus, who stocked the
works of Martial, and to whose posts advertise-
ments of new books were attached. We are told
that a cheap copy of a published work could be
bought for six or ten sesterces. We are told finally
of the fate of bad books, to be devoured by moths
or worms, to be used by cooks to wrap up meat,

or to be given as waste paper for boys to write their exercises on the back of the roll.[1]

The Imperial age, however, did not confine itself to becoming acquainted with literature through the reading of books. Another habit to which allusion is frequently made is that of public recitations. Under the Flavian emperors, in particular, this was a favourite method of securing publicity. The recitations might either be in public, in the great baths or forums, where any one might listen who chose, as to an orator in Trafalgar Square or Hyde Park, or in private houses to invited audiences. Juvenal and Petronius give us pictures of such performances. Tacitus describes how an author would be compelled to hire a house and chairs, and collect an audience by personal entreaty;[2] and Juvenal complains that a rich man would lend his disused house, and send his freedmen and poor clients to form an audience, but would not bear the cost of the chairs.[3] The whole practice finds its analogy in the modern musical world, where a singer is compelled to hire a hall and do his best to collect an audience, in order that his voice may be heard; or a patron desiring to assist him may lend his drawing-room for the purpose, and use his influence to get his

---

[1] A selection of the more important passages in the Latin poets illustrative of the production and use of books is given in the Appendix.

[2] Tacitus, *Dial.* c. 9.   [3] Juvenal, *Sat.* vii. 40–7.

friends to attend. It was not a healthy phase for literature, since it encouraged compositions which lent themselves to rhetorical declamation; and one may doubt whether it did any service to the circulation of books.

We have now briefly surveyed the history of the book throughout the golden ages of both Greek and Roman literature, and their respective declines in the Hellenistic and silver ages. Fuller particulars can be found in the standard histories of literature. Throughout this period the papyrus roll has been the dominant form of book, and of this a full description has been given in the previous chapter. But a change was at hand. A rival material was already in the field, a rival form was beginning to make itself visible, and a new literature, almost unnoticed, was coming into existence. In the next chapter we shall return to the description of the outward forms of books, and shall trace the rise of vellum as a material for books, and of the codex as their form, and their preparation both for the service of the new literature of Christianity, and for handing down the works of classical authors through the Middle Ages. The thousand years of the papyrus roll were to be succeeded by a thousand years of the vellum codex, until that in turn was to give way to the paper printed book, which has so far only enjoyed half the life of its predecessors. It is not my purpose to carry the narrative down through the Middle Ages, but the story of the transition from papyrus to vellum and from the roll to the codex is one of some importance both for classical and for Christian literature, and it is a part of the subject on which new light has been thrown by recent discoveries, which may not be without interest.

IV

VELLUM AND THE CODEX

THE subject of this chapter is the supersession of papyrus by vellum as the principal material for books, and of the roll by the codex as their form. The two processes go on side by side, and include a transitional species of book, the papyrus codex, in which the form is changed, but not the material. This was not a phenomenon of long duration, but, as will appear, it is of special interest in connexion with Christian literature, particularly the Bible. It will be convenient, and in accordance with chronology, to begin the story with the material.

The use of the skins of animals, in the form of tanned hides, or leather, has been already referred to. Vellum, or parchment, is a material also produced from skins, but by a different process and with very different results. It was prepared generally from the skins of cattle, sheep, and goats, and especially from the young of these species, calves, lambs, and kids. The skins of pigs and asses provided coarser qualities, but were not much in request. On the other hand some very fine vellum, such as that on which the celebrated Vatican and Sinaitic manuscripts are written, is said to have been derived from antelopes; but though this statement of Tischendorf's has been often repeated, it has never, so far as I know, been verified. The skins were carefully washed and scraped, so as to remove the hairs, rubbed with pumice to make them smooth, and then dressed with chalk. The result is to produce a material, almost white in colour, of great enduring power, and in the better qualities of unequalled beauty, for the reception of writing. There remains some difference between the flesh-side and the hair-side of the vellum, the latter being apt to be somewhat darker, but to retain the ink better.

The story of its invention is well known, but must be repeated as the foundation of what is to follow. The elder Pliny, in the passage dealing with the materials of books which has already been repeatedly referred to (*Nat. Hist.* xiii. 11), says, on the authority of Varro, that the origin of vellum was due to the rivalry of Ptolemy, King of Egypt, and Eumenes, King of Pergamum, as founders of libraries. He does not say which Ptolemy or which Eumenes he refers to.[1] There were two kings of the latter name, Eumenes I (263–241 B.C.) and Eumenes II (197–159 B.C.), and Ptolemies contemporary with both. Since, however, it is known that an acute rivalry existed between Eumenes II and Ptolemy Epiphanes (205–182 B.C.) in connexion with their libraries, it seems likely that they are the two sovereigns in question. Eumenes

---

[1] Sandys (*Hist. of Classical Scholarship*, i. 111) attributes it to Eumenes I; Gardthausen and Thompson to Eumenes II.

tried to steal Ptolemy's librarian, inviting Aristophanes of Byzantium, then chief of the great Alexandrian Library, to come to his court at Pergamum; whereupon Ptolemy put Aristophanes in prison.[1] He may therefore very well have taken the further step recorded by Varro, which consisted in placing an embargo on the export of papyrus. It was this embargo which led Eumenes to develop the manufacture of vellum. That its origin was traditionally attributed to Pergamum is shown by its Greek name, περγαμηνή, though this word is said not to be found earlier than the Edict of Diocletian (A.D. 301). There is also no doubt that a famous library existed at Pergamum, though there is no reason to suppose that it was eventually confined to books on vellum. A building discovered during the German excavation of the site is believed to have been its home. Pergamum, like Alexandria, became a great centre of scholarship, which, through the political association of Rome and Pergamum, had considerable influence on the development of education at Rome. According to Calvisius (a friend of Caesar's), quoted by Plutarch, the library amounted to 200,000 volumes, and was brought to an end by being presented by Antony as a gift to Cleopatra.[2]

Until recently, no example of vellum was known

---

[1] Suidas, s.v. Aristophanes. Aristophanes was librarian at Alexandria from 195 to 180 B.C.　　　　[2] *Vit. Ant.* c. 58.

which could be referred to anything like the date of Eumenes or of the Pergamum Library. Two discoveries have, however, partially filled this gap. In 1909 two documents on vellum were discovered at Avroman in Kurdistan, bearing dates equivalent to 88 and 22 B.C.;[1] and in 1923, in the course of Professor F. Cumont's excavations on the site of the Roman fortress of Dura (Salahiyeh), on the Upper Euphrates, several more vellum documents were brought to light, one of which mentions the years 117 and 123 of the era of the Seleucids, which are equivalent to 190–189 and 196–195 B.C. The vellum is of good quality, and the writing not inferior to or markedly different in style from contemporary writing on papyrus in Egypt. These documents are therefore of a date near the beginning of the reign of Eumenes II, and from a place so far distant from Pergamum that the use of this material cannot be the result of Eumenes' action. It is evident that what Eumenes did was to develop for literary purposes the use of a material already otherwise in existence.

It is not to be supposed, however, that vellum at once became a rival to papyrus in the book trade generally. It is indeed evident that it was not so. All the references in Roman literature, at least as far as the end of the first century of the

[1] Facsimiles in *Journal of Hellenic Studies*, xxxv (1915), and *New Palaeographical Society*, ii. pt. 3 (1915).

3947 N

Christian era, are plainly to papyrus. The words of Pliny (writing in the second half of the first century) imply that the use of vellum at Pergamum was merely an emergency measure at a time of difficulty, and he by no means places it on an equality with papyrus, which he regards as the principal and essential organ of human civilization and history.[1] It is true that he uses a somewhat similar phrase with regard to vellum ('postea promiscue patuit usus rei, qua constat immortalitas hominum'), which implies that it had come into widespread use in the first century; but his nephew's reference (see p. 60 above) to his 166 opisthograph volumes of extracts seems to show that his own writing was done on rolls, and he plainly regards papyrus as the more important material, worthy of the full description which he devotes to it. Vellum may have already been occupying an important secondary place in the book-world, but its main use seems to have been for note-books, which would no doubt be extensively used in the preparation of literary works, before they were consigned to papyrus for publication. Of these note-books a word must be said, since they have a bearing on the development of the codex form for books.

[1] 'Cum chartae usu maxime humanitas vitae constet et memoria' (l.c.). *Charta* is the regular word for papyrus, as appears from the context here and elsewhere in Catullus, Martial, &c.

There is frequent reference to the use of note-
books (*tabellae, pugillares*), which could be carried
on the person and used for casual annotation or
for rough copies of poems. Normally these were
of wood, coated with wax, on which writing was
inscribed with a stylus, or covered with whitewash
on which ink could be used. Martial (xiv. 3–7)
refers to several different materials used for them,
cedar-wood, ivory, and vellum (*membrana*), but
these were dainty gifts, and he implies that the
normal use was of wax. He also refers to the
combination of more than one tablet to form a
note-book (*triplices, quincuplices*). Several examples
of such tablets, plain, waxen, or whitened, survive
(e.g. B.M. Add. MSS. 33270, 33293, 37533), and
they were obviously much used for school purposes,
like slates in the nineteenth century, the wax lend-
ing itself to easy obliteration. They were also used
regularly for short letters, and could be returned
by the correspondent with his answer written on the
re-used wax. If more than one tablet was used,
they were fastened together by string or leather
thongs, and could be closed against inspection by
threads, fastened with a seal.

All these usages paved the way for the adoption
of vellum and of the codex or modern quire
formation of books, but when vellum became at all
common for literary purposes, and whether the early
Pergamum manuscripts were rolls or codices it is

difficult to say. There is, however, evidence, as we have already seen from Pliny, that towards the end of the first century of the Christian era it was quite well known, though still far from superseding papyrus. The earliest extant examples are probably two leaves, one in the British Museum containing part of Demosthenes' *De Falsa Legatione* (B.M. Add. MS. 34473 (1)), the other at Berlin containing some lines from Euripides' *Cretans* (Berl. Mus. 217), which are assigned somewhat doubtfully to the late first or second century.[1] Literary references before the end of the first century appear to be non-existent, with one exception, which needs examination. The fourteenth book of Martial's epigrams consists of couplets written (rather after the fashion of our mottoes in Christmas crackers) to accompany gifts made at the time of the Saturnalia (*apophoreta*). These, like our Christmas presents, were of all kinds—tablets, table ornaments, candlesticks, toilet instruments, a parrot, a box for a book (evidently papyrus, since the object of the case is to protect it from friction), vases of various materials, cloaks or capes, musical instruments, paintings, statuettes, and the like; but among them are thirteen which relate to books. They are as follows: Homer's *Batrachomyomachia*, 'Homerus in pugillaribus membranis', Virgil's

---

[1] Facsimiles respectively in New Pal. Soc. i, pl. 2, and ii, pl. 28.

Culex, 'Vergilius in membranis', Menander's *Thais*, 'Cicero in membranis', Propertius, 'Livius in membranis', Sallust, 'Ovidii Metamorphosis in membranis', Tibullus, Lucan, and Catullus.[1] With regard to most of these, there is no difficulty: they would be ordinary rolls of papyrus, which might be ornamented suitably for presents in the usual way. But a complete Homer (and both *Iliad* and *Odyssey* are specified), a complete Virgil, or a complete copy of the *Metamorphoses* would be a gift quite out of scale with the other presents recorded; while a Christmas present of a complete Livy in 142 books is a *reductio ad absurdum*. Moreover the epigrams themselves imply that something quite small is intended. The Homer is expressly said to be in a note-book. Of the Virgil he says:

Quam brevis immensum cepit membrana Maronem!

and of the Livy:

Pellibus exiguis arctatur Livius ingens,
    quem mea non totum bibliotheca capit.

It is evident from this that these were not ordinary copies of the authors named, but were miniatures of some sort, presumably either extracts or epitomes. It is observable also that in each case the fact that they are 'in membranis' is explicitly stated. This in itself implies that they are not books of the usual kind. These references therefore

[1] See Appendix for the complete text.

cannot be used as evidence that vellum codices
were in common circulation in Martial's time, at
the end of the first century. So far the evidence
goes to show that up to the date which we have
reached, the papyrus roll remained the normal and
dominant form of book.

It is now time to take up the story of the papyrus
codex, the application of the codex form to the
papyrus material. Until quite recently the evidence for this has been scanty. Among the papyri
found in Egypt there have been instances, relatively
few but sufficient to establish the fact, of papyrus
manuscripts in codex form. For the most part they
were of late date, and several were Coptic works.
The most important was the manuscript of four
plays of Menander, discovered at Kom Ishgau by
G. Lefebvre in 1905, and datable probably to the
fifth century. Other Greek papyrus codices of
some size were a manuscript of part of the Minor
Prophets at Heidelberg, of the seventh century;[1]
a finely written copy of St. Cyril of Alexandria,
De Adoratione, partly at Dublin and partly at Paris,
of the same century;[2] several books of magic in
the British Museum and in Paris, of the fourth
century; seven leaves of Callimachus' *Aetia* and
Iambi from Oxyrhynchus, of the end of the fourth

[1] Published with facsimile by Deissmann, *Veröffentlichungen aus
der Heidelberger Papyrus-sammlung*, 1905.
[2] Facsimile in New. Pal. Soc. i, pl. 203.

century; and several copies of parts of Homer. With the exception of the Cyril, they are inferior specimens of book-production, written in rough hands on coarse papyrus, and represent a stage when papyrus had definitely taken an inferior position to vellum in the book trade. The earliest in date was a manuscript of Homer, *Iliad* ii–iv, in the British Museum (B.M. pap. 126), which is apparently of the third century. This is written on one side only of each leaf, as if the scribe was not accustomed to the codex technique, and did not realize its advantages. In addition there were a considerable number of smaller fragments, none of them earlier than the third century, which could be shown from the arrangement of the text on both sides to have come from codices.

One remarkable point to which attention was gradually drawn as more examples came to light was that the contents of these papyrus codices, and especially of the earlier ones, were predominantly Christian. Among them were many Biblical fragments, and the celebrated Oxyrhynchus papyrus of the *Sayings of Jesus*. Statistics showed a striking discrepancy in the proportions of the roll and codex forms as between pagan and Christian works. An examination of all the manuscripts from Oxyrhynchus up to the year 1926 gave the following results. Before the third century no codices appeared at all. In the third century, out of 106 manuscripts containing pagan literature, a hundred were rolls and only six codices; while of seventeen containing Christian works only seven were rolls, while eight were papyrus codices and two vellum codices. In the fourth century there is a great drop in the output of pagan literature. Only fourteen manuscripts belonged to this category, and of these six were rolls, three were papyrus codices, and five vellum codices. Christian works were by now in a majority, being thirty-six in all; and of these all were codices, with the exception of one schoolboy's exercise, and a copy of the Epistle to the Hebrews written on the back of an Epitome of Livy. Of the thirty-four codices, twenty-one are on papyrus and thirteen on vellum. Papyrus still predominates in Egypt, but the roll is almost extinct, and the vogue of vellum is increasing. From the fifth century there were twenty-five pagan manuscripts, of which only four were rolls, while there were seventeen papyrus codices and four vellum codices; among twenty-one Christian manuscripts there were four rolls, seven papyrus codices, and ten vellum codices. From the sixth century the total number of literary texts hitherto produced from Oxyrhynchus was much smaller. Of six pagan manuscripts two were rolls, three papyrus codices, and one a vellum codex; while of eight Christian manuscripts two were rolls, five papyrus codices, and one a vellum codex.

The conclusions to which these figures led, which were supported by the discoveries from other sites, though the figures for them have not been tabulated, plainly was that in the third century, and to a less extent in the fourth, the roll was in an overwhelming majority for pagan works, while the codex had a decided and growing majority for Christian works. It was therefore fair to attribute to the Christians a considerable share in the introduction of the codex form of book-manufacture; and this seemed to explain itself as a corollary of the fact, previously indicated, that vellum was at first and for some time regarded as an inferior material for the purpose. The Christian community was a poor one, and subject to periodical persecution, and it is not likely that they were often able to command the services of the best professional scribes. It seemed, therefore, as if the origin of the papyrus codex was to be looked for in the third century, and its vogue to be found principally in Christian circles.

Recently, however, a flood of new light has been thrown on the papyrus codex from a discovery which was announced in November, 1931. This was a group of papyri obtained in Egypt (the exact place of discovery has not been revealed) by Mr. A. Chester Beatty. It consists of twelve manuscripts, all on papyrus, all codices, and all containing Christian literature—in all probability the remains of the library of some early church or monastery. Their dates can only be fixed on palaeographical grounds, but they appear to range from the second to the fourth or fifth century. None is perfect, but most contain substantial portions of the books that they represent. Eight contain portions of the Old Testament; two of Genesis, one of Numbers and Deuteronomy, one of Ezekiel and Esther (written in different hands in the same volume), one of Isaiah, one of Jeremiah, one of Daniel (in the original Septuagint version, of which only one other copy is known), and one of Ecclesiasticus. Three are of the New Testament: one which contained originally all the four Gospels and the Acts (a phenomenon of considerable importance, as will appear presently), one of all or the greater part of the Pauline Epistles, and one of Revelation. Finally, one contains portions of the lost Greek original of the Book of Enoch and one or more Christian homilies. All, as said before, are codices, and contain sufficient remains of their page numeration to make it possible to calculate their original length, and in most cases to determine their make-up in quires.

This addition of new material greatly increases the volume of evidence for the conclusions already expressed, confirming them in bulk, but also extending and modifying them in some directions.

It confirms emphatically the early use of the codex
form by the Christian community; indeed it shows
that it was even earlier than there had hitherto
been any ground to believe. It is true that the
dating of the Chester Beatty Papyri has to be
determined solely on palaeographical grounds, and
consequently that there is room for differences of
opinion; but with regard to the earliest of the
manuscripts, that which contains Numbers and
Deuteronomy, it does not appear possible to place
it later than the second century, or even than
about the middle of that century. If that be accepted (as it is by others besides myself) the origin
of the papyrus codex and its use at any rate by
Christians is brought back to somewhere near the
beginning of the second century. It is to be observed also that this particular manuscript is the
best written of the whole group. It is the work of
a trained scribe, which shows either that the
Christians occasionally could command the services of such, or that this manuscript was produced
for the Jewish community (who would not be
restricted either by poverty or by persecution)
before it passed into its present Christian company.

A consequence of considerable importance for
Biblical criticism follows. Since a papyrus roll, as
already shown, could not contain more than a
single Gospel, and there was hitherto no evidence
of the use of the codex before the third century,

it. was not only permissible but necessary to con-
clude that before the third century at earliest there
could have been no such thing as a collected New
Testament, and that even the four Gospels could
not have been gathered into a single volume, but
must have circulated only in separate rolls. This
made it easy to understand, for example, the lesser
knowledge shown of St. Mark in early writers as
compared with the other Gospels. The Chester
Beatty Papyri modify this conclusion materially. It
is still probable that the several Gospels often circulated separately, but it is no longer possible to assert
that they could not have been known as a com-
bined whole in the second century. The Gospels
and Acts manuscript in the collection may probably
be assigned to the third century, and so also the
manuscript of the Pauline Epistles; but the Numbers and Deuteronomy manuscript shows that the
codex form was in use in the preceding century;
hence it is now possible that Irenaeus, to whom
the four Gospels stood apart by themselves as a
record of the Saviour's life, knew them as a single
volume, and that Origen may have had such a
volume at his command, whether at Alexandria
or at Caesarea.

It is now time to describe the external appearance and make-up of the papyrus codex. It was
no doubt modelled on the form of the note-books,
whether of wood or of vellum, which have already

been described; but there is an essential difference between the treatment of vellum and papyrus in forming the sheets or quires of a codex. A large skin of vellum could be, and habitually was, folded in both directions, vertically and horizontally, and therefore formed quires of 2, 4, 8, or 16 leaves, just as is the case with paper to-day. Papyrus, however, was not tall enough to fold in more than one direction, and the same sheet could not be folded more than once without risk of splitting or tearing. Consequently the method of forming a papyrus codex was to take a number of sheets, each twice the size of the required page, and to fold them once in the middle. A single sheet would thus form two leaves, or four pages; and the simplest form of codex would be formed of a succession of such single-sheet quires. But a number of sheets could be laid, one on top of another, and the whole folded at once; and in this way a quire could be formed containing twice as many leaves as there were sheets before the folding. Any multiple of two is therefore possible as the number of leaves in a quire of papyrus. Now there had been some evidence previously of a practice of forming very large quires in this manner. Among the early discoveries at Oxyrhynchus was a sheet of papyrus (P. Oxy. 208), attributable from the writing to the third century, forming two leaves of a codex, with a portion of chapter i

of St. John's Gospel on the first leaf, and a portion
of chapter xx on the other. This implied that the
sheet was nearly the outermost one in a large
quire, which originally contained the entire Gospel.
Calculation showed that this involved a quire
composed of 25 sheets, forming, when folded, 50
leaves or 100 pages; the whole being held together
by threads passed through holes pierced in a
vertical line down the centre of the sheets. The
whole codex thus formed a single quire.[1]

On the other hand some of the other extant
codices showed a different method, more like that
of a vellum codex. Examples were few, since most
of the relics of codices were single leaves, affording
no evidence of their original quire-formation; but
a few substantial codices were known. Of these,
the Menander codex (5th cent.) seems to have
quires of 8 leaves, the Cyril (7th cent.) the same,
and the Heidelberg Minor Prophets (7th cent.)
to have varied between 8 and 10. It will be
observed, however, that all these are of relatively
late date, after the vellum technique had become
well established.

The Chester Beatty Papyri greatly amplify the
available evidence, and show examples of all the

---

[1] A Coptic example of the same formation, and consisting
likewise of 50 leaves, occurs in the manuscript of St. John's
Gospel discovered by Sir Flinders Petrie and edited by Sir
Herbert Thompson among the publications of the British School
of Archaeology in Egypt (1924).

methods of codex-formation that have been mentioned. The Gospels and Acts manuscript was formed of a succession of single-sheet quires, i.e. of quires of two leaves, being the only certain example of this form. Three of them, the Isaiah, the Ezekiel and Esther, and the Pauline Epistles, were certainly composed of single quires of large size; and two others, the Daniel and the Revelation, probably were so. The page numeration makes it possible to calculate, at any rate with approximate accuracy, the original size of the codex when complete. From this it appears that the Isaiah was a codex formed of a single quire of 112 leaves (i.e. 56 sheets of papyrus, folded in the middle), and the Pauline Epistles similarly was a single quire of about 92 leaves. The Ezekiel and Esther codex appears to have had about 78 leaves. The Daniel manuscript (for a reason which will appear later) was probably also a single-quire codex, of approximately 96 leaves, with some other books preceding Daniel. The Revelation manuscript was either composed of three quires, of 12, 10, and 10 leaves respectively, or (perhaps more probably) of a single quire of 32 leaves.

On the other hand two manuscripts, the second Genesis and the Enoch, are certainly examples of codex-formation in a series of small quires, the Genesis being composed of quires of 10 leaves, and the Enoch of 12. Of two more manuscripts, the Ecclesiasticus and the Jeremiah, the remains are too small for their structure to be ascertainable; while the formation of the remaining two, the first Genesis and the Numbers and Deuteronomy, is doubtful for another reason, arising from another feature of the papyrus codex, which has still to be explained.

When a number of sheets of papyrus were to be formed into a codex, as explained above, the natural method was to lay them one above the other, with the *recto* side uppermost in each case. When the set of sheets was then folded in the middle to form a quire, it is obvious that in the first half of the quire so formed the *verso* side of each leaf would precede the *recto*, while in the second half the *recto* would precede the *verso*. This is so in the case of all the Chester Beatty codices of which the quire formation has just been described. It is because in all the extant leaves of the Daniel the *recto* precedes the *verso* that it is practically certain that they belong to the second half of a large quire; and it is because *verso* precedes *recto* in the Ezekiel and *recto verso* in the Esther that it may be presumed that Ezekiel came first in that manuscript. A consequence of this method of forming the quire, however, was that at every opening of the book (except at the middles and ends of the quires) the page on one side of the opening would have its fibres vertical (*verso*) while on the other the fibres would be horizontal (*recto*). If it was desired to avoid this lack of uniformity, it was necessary to dispose the sheets, before they were folded to form a quire, with *recto* and *verso* uppermost alternately. If this were done, *recto* would face *recto*, and *verso* *verso*, at each opening of the book.

This result can be achieved with quires of any size, from two leaves upwards, and with fragmentary manuscripts so arranged there are no means of deciding the size of the quires unless actual conjugate leaves are preserved. In the Gospels and Acts manuscript this is in fact the case, and we can prove that it was composed of a number of 2-leaf quires; but in the larger Genesis and the Numbers and Deuteronomy there are no conjugate leaves, and we are therefore left without evidence. In them *recto* pages face *recto* and *verso* *verso* throughout the book; but there is nothing to prove whether they were single-quire codices like the Isaiah and others or had quires of medium size (10 or 12 leaves) like the second Genesis and Enoch, or small 2-leaf quires like the Gospels and Acts manuscript.

It may be observed that the method of forming quires with pages of like character facing one another occurs also in vellum codices, where hair-side pages face hair-side and flesh-side flesh-side; but there it happens naturally, as any one can

ascertain by experiment, in the double or quadru-
plicate folding of a large skin. Whether the application of this practice to papyrus was the result of
an imitation of the vellum technique, or was
arrived at independently on aesthetic grounds,
cannot be determined.

There are therefore the following various possi-
bilities in the formation of a papyrus codex: (1) A
single large quire, which may be of as many leaves
as can be folded without excessive inconvenience;
in this the *verso* pages will precede the *recto* in the
first half of the codex, while *recto* will precede *verso*
in the second half. (Obviously the opposite result
could be obtained if all the sheets, before folding,
were laid with the *verso* uppermost; and this is
found in some Coptic codices mentioned below,
but not in any Greek manuscript known to me.)
(2) A succession of quires of a small number of
leaves, usually 8 or 10 or 12, in which *verso*
precedes *recto* in the first half of each quire, and
recto verso in the second half. (3) A succession of
quires of only 2 leaves, formed by the folding of
a single sheet of papyrus; technically this is only
a special case of the preceding category, but it has
the effect of making *recto* pages face *recto*, and *verso*
verso, throughout the codex, which is not the case
with either of the two previous methods. (4) A
single large quire in which the sheets before folding
have been laid with *recto* and *verso* alternately upper-

most, so that *recto* pages face *recto* and *verso* *verso* throughout the codex. (5) A succession of small quires similarly arranged. Examples of nos. 1, 2, and 3 occur among the Chester Beatty Papyri. The two uncertain manuscripts may belong to nos. 3, 4, or 5, but (at any rate so far as investigation has hitherto gone) it is impossible to say which. An example of no. 5 is found in the Cairo Menander codex, and in the greater part of the British Museum Coptic Psalter (Or. 5000).

The existing evidence is not sufficient to make it possible to trace the chronological development of the papyrus codex. It would seem probable, however, that both the large single-quire form and the 2-leaf quire were early experiments, which eventually gave way to the quires of 8 or 10 or 12 leaves. This is to some extent borne out by the fact that all the later papyrus codices (5th–7th cent.) are of the latter kind. In any case it is not likely that there was any hard and fast line of chronological demarcation between the styles.[1]

[1] All the Greek papyrus codices known to me are regular in their quire-formation according to one or other of the methods described. Coptic codices, on the other hand, appear to have been made up with a considerable lack of method. Mr. Crum (*Journal of Theological Studies*, xi. 301) describes three important manuscripts, all now in the British Museum. One (Or. 5984), containing the Sapiential books (edited by Sir H. Thompson), has quires of 8 leaves, with *recto* preceding *verso* in the first half, and *verso* preceding *recto* in the second; from which it follows that the sheets before folding were laid with the *verso* uppermost. The

To complete the description of the papyrus codices known to us, something should be said as to their dimensions. The great Menander codex at Cairo has pages of $12\frac{1}{4} \times 7\frac{1}{8}$ inches. Another codex of Menander, of which there is a leaf at Geneva, measured $11\frac{1}{8} \times 6\frac{3}{4}$ inches. The Cyril at Paris and Dublin measures $12 \times 8\frac{1}{2}$ inches; the Minor Prophets at Heidelberg about $10\frac{1}{2} \times 6\frac{1}{2}$ inches. The Coptic Gospel of St. John discovered by Sir Flinders Petrie is 10×5 inches. Some Coptic codices in the British Museum are larger. That which contains the Sapiential Books (Or. 5984) measures as much as $14\frac{1}{4} \times 10\frac{1}{2}$ inches; the Psalter (Or. 5000) $11\frac{3}{4} \times 8\frac{1}{2}$ inches; the volume of Homilies (Or. 5001), $12\frac{3}{4} \times 9$ inches; a codex containing Deuteronomy, Jonah, and Acts (Or. 7594) about

second (Or. 5000, edited by Sir E. Budge), a Psalter, has 20 quires, 18 being of 8 leaves, in which the first has the following arrangement: *r–v, r–v, r–v, v–r: r–v, v–r, v–r, v–r*, and the second *v–r, v–r, r–v, v–r: r–v, v–r, r–v, v–r* (since the first and last of these are both *v–r*, they must have been two separate leaves, artificially joined, not a single folded sheet); then follow 16 quires in which *r–v* and *v–r* alternate regularly; then follow 2 smaller quires, one of 6 leaves (*r–v, v–r, v–r, r–v, r–v, v–r*), and one of 4 (*r–v, v–r, r–v, r–v*). The arrangment is not quite correctly stated by Mr. Crum. The third (Or. 5001), a collection of Homilies, has quires of 8 leaves, very irregularly arranged. In two only does *recto* precede regularly in the first half and *verso* in the second: all the rest have varying sequences, showing that the sheets before folding were laid at haphazard.

It is to be observed, however, that all these Coptic codices are of relatively late date, and can by no means be regarded as high-class examples of book-production.

$12\frac{1}{2}\times6\frac{1}{2}$ inches. The Chester Beatty MSS. are for the most part smaller. In four cases the original size of the leaf appears to have been about 11×7 inches, while four others are approximately 11×6, 10×8, $9\frac{1}{2}\times5\frac{1}{2}$, and 8×7 inches. Two of them, however, the Daniel and the Ezekiel and Esther, were of a very unusual shape, exceptionally tall and narrow, measuring about 14×5 inches. The measurements of the remaining two are uncertain, but in the Isaiah the width of the leaf is 6 inches. In nearly all papyrus codices, both Chester Beatty and others, there is only one column of writing to the page; but the larger Genesis manuscript and the Numbers and Deuteronomy have double columns. In the latter case the columns are very narrow, being only about 2 inches wide; and considering the date of this manuscript, this may be an imitation of the narrow columns usual in papyrus rolls.

I have dealt at length and in some detail with the form and history of the papyrus codex both because of the novelty of some of the information and because of its importance, now more than ever evident, in connexion with early Christian litera-ture. It will be seen that according to the evidence hitherto available, it was the predominant form of book among the Christians in Egypt in the third and fourth centuries, and that it was known in the second; though it is fair to point out that this last statement rests on the date which I have assigned to the Numbers and Deuteronomy manuscript. In quality of material and workmanship, it does not (except in the case of this same manuscript and of the late copy of St. Cyril) rank very high, and it is evident that at any rate up to the end of the third century it ranked lower in the book trade than the papyrus roll. In the fourth century both papyrus roll and papyrus codex succumbed to the vellum codex, as will be shown shortly.

It is now necessary to return to pagan literature, and to complete the story of the papyrus roll. It has, I hope, been made clear that up to the end of the first century the papyrus roll was completely dominant, and that the evidence of Martial's Christmas presents proves nothing to the contrary. The same appears to be true of the second century. Among all the papyri discovered in Egypt which can be assigned to the second century (and it will be remembered that the second and third centuries are far more plentifully represented than any other) no single pagan manuscript (and hitherto only one or perhaps two Christian manuscripts) is in codex form.

For the centuries that follow, the statistics given on pp. 95, 96 can be supplemented from an examination of Oldfather's list, which it will be remembered deals only with pagan literature, but in that respect covers the whole papyrological field and is not confined to Oxyrhynchus. Treating the dates as given in that list in the same way as before, and with the same caution as to the unreliability of some of them, the results are as follows. Of the 304 manuscripts assigned to the third century, 275 are papyrus rolls; only 26 are papyrus codices and 3 vellum codices. In the fourth century, on the other hand, out of a total of 83, 34 are papyrus codices, and 10 vellum codices. In the fifth century, out of a total of 78, 55 are codices, 43 being papyrus and 12 vellum. In the sixth century, out of a total of 29, 14 are codices, 10 being papyrus and 4 vellum. In the seventh century, out of a total of 13, 5 are papyrus codices and 6 vellum.

From these figures it appears that in considering the textual history of a pagan author the codex barely comes into consideration for the third century, less than a tenth of the whole number being in this form, and some of these being probably school or private copies. For Christian authors, on the other hand, the codex form is probable (though not universal) for the third century and admissible for the second, though we cannot yet say whether it was then normal or exceptional.

The decline of papyrus is definitely to be dated from the fourth century. The reason for the somewhat abrupt change is not quite clear, but two causes may have co-operated, one being a demand for volumes of a greater bulk than the papyrus

roll, and the other an improvement in the manufacture of vellum. The adoption of Christianity as
the official religion of the Roman Empire no doubt
led to a demand for copies of its official Scriptures.
We know that Constantine ordered fifty copies for
his new capital alone, and the Empire as a whole
must have required thousands. It would have been
inconvenient to supply these in roll form; moreover a collection of rolls furnished no evidence of
completeness, while a codex formed a unit in itself.
Hence it is at this period that we find the limits of
the Canon being fixed, and complete Bibles being
produced for the first time. The experience of the
papyrus codex had shown that a far greater extent
of text could be included in a single codex than
in a single roll. The Chester Beatty MS. shows
that the four Gospels and the Acts could be contained in a single codex, whereas they would have
occupied five distinct rolls. Moreover, a codex
could be increased almost indefinitely without
becoming unmanageable, while a roll was in-
creasingly inconvenient to handle as it grew in
length. The only drawback might have been the
difficulty of binding. The single-quire papyrus
codex could not be increased beyond the 50 sheets
or thereabouts of which we have examples, without
becoming too fat to fold. It was therefore necessary to use the smaller kind of quire, of 8 or 10
leaves, which would have to be sewn together

inside some form of cover: and here there would be some tendency of the papyrus to tear away from the stitching with age and use. The obvious remedy was to use vellum. It is probable that the technique of preparing vellum had improved during the centuries that had passed since its invention, and the literary world was prepared for the discovery that it provided a material no less attractive to the eye than papyrus and much more durable, in addition to the advantage of being able to include within a single cover as much text as any one could wish to combine into a unit.

A further consideration which may have had some effect is the greater convenience of reference afforded by the codex. As was described in a previous chapter, very little consideration was shown for the convenience of readers in the papyrus roll. It must have been excessively inconvenient to have to unroll and roll up one's manuscript constantly when in search of particular passages; and this inconvenience may have something to do with the inexactitude of quotations in classical authors. So long as only works of ordinary literature were concerned, this might not matter much; but when it was a question of dealing with works on which the salvation of the soul depended, references to the authoritative texts were more needful, and accuracy of quotation was more essential. The same considerations would also apply to some extent to the collections of laws which became common under the Empire. A form of book which could be consulted by merely turning the leaves obviously had a great advantage over a roll. In this connexion it may also be noted that a system of numbered sections was introduced in the books of the New Testament, which answered the purpose of the much later division into chapters and verses; though Christian literature does not, so far as I know, contain any examples of the citation of texts by means of this numeration.

The above-mentioned considerations, then, of comprehensiveness, durability, and convenience of reference may reasonably be regarded as accounting satisfactorily for the ultimate victory of the codex over the roll and of vellum over papyrus. Of the main fact that in the fourth century vellum took the place of papyrus as the principal material for the best book-production there can be no question. There is evidence for it both external and internal. Jerome, in an often-quoted passage (Ep. 141), records that the papyrus volumes in the library of Pamphilus at Caesarea, which had become damaged, were replaced by copies on vellum.[1] This was about the year 350. Before this, Constantine had ordered his fifty copies for Con-

----

[1] 'Quam [bibliothecam] ex parte corruptam Acacius dehinc et Euzoius, eiusdem ecclesiae sacerdotes, in membranis instaurare conati sunt.'

stantinople, and these are expressly said to have been on vellum (πεντήκοντα σωμάτια ἐν διφθέραις). And it is to about this same period that the two great volumes which head the roll of vellum manuscripts of the Greek Bible, the Codex Vaticanus and the Codex Sinaiticus, are to be referred. After the production of books so beautiful as these, containing in a single volume of not excessive size the whole of the canonical Scriptures (even with the addition of some doubtful books), no one could doubt that the victory of the vellum codex was complete.

It is not perhaps irrelevant to note that these two earliest specimens of the new fashion show traces of having been copied from rolls rather than from codices. This appears in the narrowness of the columns used. The Vatican MS. has three narrow columns to its page, the Sinaitic, with its wider page, has four, which exactly reproduce the effect of the columns in a papyrus roll. Further experience showed the advantage of a wider column; and by the fifth century the Codex Alexandrinus has the arrangement with two columns to the page, which thenceforth became normal (with an occasional experiment in single columns) in the large vellum manuscripts.

Vellum appears also to have been adopted at about the same time for secular works. The dating of early vellum uncial manuscripts is a precarious task, since few fixed points are available. Moreover it would appear that the scribes who set the fashion in the use of the new material modelled themselves on the best examples known to them on papyrus, which were those of the second century; much as the scribes and printers of the Italian Renaissance modelled themselves on the Carolingian manuscripts of the ninth and tenth centuries. The Vatican and Sinaitic MSS. of the Greek Bible, which cannot be earlier than the fourth century, recall the papyri of the second; and similarly the Ambrosian MS. of the *Iliad* at Milan is in a hand extraordinarily like those of two second-century papyri of the same poem, though it can itself hardly be placed earlier than the third century. Early Latin uncials are even more difficult to date than Greek; but there is a group of manuscripts of Virgil, including those known as the Vatican, Medicean, and Palatine, which are certainly not later than the fifth century, and which modern criticism is inclined to place at least as early as the fourth. To the fourth century also probably belong such Latin vellum manuscripts as the Vercelli Gospels and the palimpsest of Cicero *De Republica*. In Latin as in Greek, in secular as in Christian texts, the supremacy of vellum as a writing material may be definitely dated from the fourth century.

Papyrus, however, did not wholly go out of use, especially in the land of its origin. Although the

output of works of literature falls abruptly in the
fourth century, as indicated above, it by no means
ceases. Throughout the fourth, fifth, and sixth
centuries papyrus manuscripts still appear among
the Egyptian ruins and rubbish-heaps, and some
very valuable additions to our knowledge have
been made from them, notably in respect of
Menander and Callimachus. The falling-off in
quantity seems to indicate a reduction in literary
culture, and the falling-off in quality of material
and writing indicates the lower position now
taken by papyrus. Nevertheless, even at the end
of the fourth century, and in a country far removed
from Egypt, we find Augustine apologizing for
using vellum for a letter, in place of either papyrus
or his private tablets, which he has dispatched
elsewhere.[1]

With the fourth century, however, we are
definitely reaching the end of one age and the
beginning of another, in the reading as well as
the writing of books. It is true that throughout the
fourth century literary culture was the mark of
the higher classes of Roman society. Withdrawn
more and more from active political life, the
Roman gentry cultivated literary studies with

[1] *Ep. ad Romanianum* (Migne, *Patr. Lat.* xxxiii. 80): 'Non haec
epistola sic inopiam chartae indicat, ut membranas saltem abun-
dare testetur [?testatur]. Tabellas eburneas quas habeo avun-
culo tuo cum litteris misi. Tu enim huic pelliculae facilius
ignosces, quia differri non potuit quod ei scripsi.'

genuine zeal. The original productiveness of the age was not great, and had little merit, with the notable exceptions of Ausonius ʳand Claudian; but the letters of Symmachus and the *Saturnalia* of Macrobius show us how widely the ancient authors were read, and how minutely they were studied. Especially was there a strong taste for rhetorical compositions, which are convincing evidence alike of an interest in literary study and of a lamentable lack of both taste and original capacity. Still, our present concern is with books and reading; and through the fourth century the books of pagan literature were extensively read, and presumably also copied, in the dwindling society of the Roman aristocracy.[1]

That society, however, was not a large one. It was spread thinly over the western Empire, in Africa, in Spain, and especially at this period in Gaul; but it did not touch the main mass of the population, in which the knowledge of the pagan literature took little root. We have no reason to suppose that books were extensively produced or read outside the narrow society of cultured Romans, except so far as a new literature was growing up around the Christian Church. In that Church some of the leading writers, such as Jerome especially and to a lesser extent Augustine,

---

[1] See Dill, *Roman Society in the last century of the Western Empire,* especially Books II and V.

were deeply steeped in pagan literature; but it was with a doubtful conscience, and almost against their will, that they accepted the influence of Virgil and Cicero. The Church as a whole did not encourage pagan literature; pagan literature had ceased to perpetuate itself and to put out fresh growth; and pagan literature died, except as the study of the society which still remained pagan at heart, whatever it might be in profession.

It was, however, a dying society, and when it disappeared beneath the barbarian invasions, there was no reading public in the old sense left. A new reading public had to be created, by a long and laborious process, through the medium of the Church and the monasteries, and dominated by the Christian religion and Christian thought, with the knowledge of classical literature maintaining a fitful and difficult existence, until the Renaissance. This period of a thousand years corresponds almost exactly with the dominance of the vellum book, a book capable of the greatest magnificence and beauty that books have ever reached, but with a history of its own, and with a character and qualities very different from those of the papyrus book that we have been considering, which for the thousand years of its reign was the vehicle of the literatures of Greece and Rome, as for an even longer period it had been the vehicle of the literature of Egypt.

APPENDIX

ILLUSTRATIVE PASSAGES FROM LATIN AUTHORS

The materials of books, and especially papyrus.

Pliny, *Nat. Hist.* xiii. cc. 11, 12.

Prius tamen quam digrediamur ab Aegypto, et papyri natura dicetur, cum chartae usu maxime humanitas vitae constet et memoria. Et hanc Alexandri Magni victoria repertam auctor est M. Varro, condita in Aegypto Alexandria. Antea non fuisse chartarum usum; in palmarum foliis primo scriptitatum, deinde quarundam arborum libris; postea publica monumenta plumbeis voluminibus, mox et privata linteis confici coepta, aut ceris; pugillarium enim usum fuisse etiam ante Troiana tempora invenimus apud Homerum.... Mox aemulatione circa bibliothecas regum Ptolemaei et Eumenis, supprimente chartas Ptolemaeo, idem Varro membranas Pergami tradidit repertas; postea promiscue patuit usus rei qua constat immortalitas hominum.

Papyrum ergo nascitur in palustribus Aegypti, aut quiescentibus Nili aquis, ubi evagatae stagnant, duo cubita non excedente altitudine gurgitum, brachiali radicis obliquae crassitudine, triangulis lateribus, decem non amplius cubitorum longitudine, in gracilitatem fastigatum thyrsi modo cacumen includens.
... Radicibus incolae pro ligno utuntur: nec ignis tantum gratia, sed ad alia quoque utensilia vasorum. Ex ipso quidem papyro navigia texunt, et e libro vela tegetesque, nec non et vestem, etiam stragulam ac funes.... Nuper et in Euphrate nascens circa Babylonem papyrum intellectum est eundem

usum habere chartae, et tamen adhuc malunt Parthi vestibus literas intexere.

Praeparantur ex eo chartae, diviso acu in praetenues sed quam latissimas philuras. Principatus medio, atque inde scissurae ordine. Hieratica appellabatur antiquitus, religiosis tantum voluminibus dicata; quae ab adulatione Augusti nomen accepit, sicut secunda Liviae a coniuge eius; ita descendit hieratica in tertium nomen. Proximum amphitheatricae datum fuerat a confecturae loco. Excepit hanc Romae Fannii sagax officina, tenuatamque curiosa interpolatione principalem fecit e plebeia, et nomen ei dedit: quae non esset ita recurata, in suo mansit amphitheatrica. Post hanc Saitica, ab oppido ubi maxima fertilitas; ex vilioribus ramentis, propiorque etiamnum cortici, Taeniotica a vicino loco, pondere iam haec, non bonitate, venalis. Nam emporetica inutilis scribendo, involucris chartarum, segestriumque in mercibus usum praebet, ideo a mercatoribus cognominatur. . . .

Texuntur omnes tabulae madentes [*al.* tabula madente] Nili aqua; turbidus liquor vim glutini praebet, cum primo supina tabula scheda adlinitur longitudine papyri quae potuit esse, resegminibus utrinque amputatis, transversa postea crates peragit. Premitur deinde praelis, et siccantur sole plagulae, atque inter se iunguntur, proximarum semper bonitatis diminutione ad deterrimas. Numquam plures scapo quam vicenae. Magna in latitudine earum differentia: tredecim digitorum optimis; duo detrahuntur hieraticae; Fanniana denos habet, et uno minus amphitheatrica; pauciores Saitica, nec malleo sufficit; nam emporeticae brevitas sex digitos non excedit.

'Before passing from Egypt, something should be said with regard to papyrus, since in the use of this material the culture and history of mankind are pre-eminently embodied. Marcus Varro is our authority for the statement that it was discovered as the result of the victories of Alexander the Great, after his foundation of Alexandria in Egypt. Before that date (he says) papyrus books were not used. In primitive ages writing was first inscribed on palm-leaves, and next on the bark of certain trees. Subsequently public documents were consigned to rolls of lead, and presently private writings also were committed to linen or to wax: for we learn from Homer that the use of tablets was known even before the Trojan War. . . . Later, as a result of the rivalry between kings Ptolemy and Eumenes over their respective libraries, when Ptolemy prohibited the export of papyrus, vellum books (again according to Varro) were invented at Pergamum; and thereafter the use of the material spread generally, so that it has become the vehicle of human immortality.

'To return to papyrus. It grows in the marshes of Egypt and in the stagnant waters of the inundations of the Nile. The depth of water in which it grows does not exceed two cubits. Its root has the thickness of a man's arm, with a triangular section. Its height is not more than ten cubits, ending in a feathery top, like a thyrsus. . . . The natives use the root as a substitute for wood, not merely as fuel, but for the manufacture of vessel utensils. Of the plant itself they weave boats, and of the bark they make sails and roof-coverings, also garments, rugs, and ropes. . . . Of late it is understood that papyrus growing in the Euphrates about Babylon has been similarly used as writing material, though the Parthians still prefer to weave letters in their garments.

'The method of preparation of the writing material from papyrus is as follows. It is divided with a needle into strips, exceedingly thin but as wide as possible. The best quality is provided by the strips from the middle (of the stem), the next to these following in order of merit. The best was originally called *hieratica* [i.e. priestly], and was reserved for works of religion. To this the name of *Augusta* was given, out of compliment to the Emperor, just as the second quality had its name from his consort Livia. The term *hieratica* was accordingly relegated to the third place. The next received the name of *amphitheatrica*, from the place of its manufacture. The ingenious manufactory of Fannius at Rome took this over, refined it by a skilful admixture of materials, made it an article of prime instead of vulgar quality, and gave it its own name [sc. *Fanniana*]: the fabric which had not been so treated retained its former status as *amphitheatrica*. Next after this comes *Saitica*, from the town where it is produced most freely. *Taeniotica* (so called from a neighbouring town) is made out of the inferior material, near the bark, and is sold only by weight, not by quality. *Emporetica* [the lowest grade] is useless for writing purposes, and is employed for book-covers and wrappings for commercial purposes; whence it gets its name. . . .

'The sheets are soaked during the process of fabrication in Nile water [or 'the fabrication is conducted on a board running with Nile water']; for this turbid fluid adds strength to the glue [*al.* vim glutinis praebet, 'has

the effect of glue']. A layer is first laid out on a flat
board of the width for which the papyrus-fibres suffice.
Its edges are trimmed, and then another layer is super-
imposed at right angles to it. It is then pressed in
a pressing-machine, the sheets are dried in the sun,
and are then attached to one another, the qualities
being arranged in descending order of merit. There
are never more than twenty sheets in a roll. The width
of sheets differs greatly; the best qualities have a
width of 13 digits [about 9¾ in.]; *hieratica* two less,
Fanniana 10, *amphitheatrica* 9: *Saitica* has less, and is
not strong enough to stand hammering. *Emporetica*,
the narrowest, does not exceed 6 digits.'

The remaining particulars given by Pliny are not
of sufficient interest in this connexion to warrant

The form of books.

Catullus, i. 1–6.

> Quoi dono lepidum novum libellum
> Arida modo pumice expolitum?
> Corneli, tibi; namque tu solebas
> Meas esse aliquid putare nugas,
> Iam tum cum ausus es, unus Italorum,
> Omne aevum tribus explicare chartis.

> 6. *Tribus chartis*: i.e. in three rolls.

Martial, viii. 72.

> Nondum murice cultus asperoque
> Morsu pumicis aridi politus,
> Arcanum properas sequi, libelle.

Martial, iii. 2. 7–11.

> Cedro nunc licet ambules perunctus,
> Et frontis gemino decens honore

Pictis luxurieris umbilicis,
Et te purpura delicata velet,
Et cocco rubeat superbus index.

Martial v. 6. 12–15.

Non est quod metuas preces iniquas :
Numquam grandia nec molesta poscit
Quae cedro decorata purpuraque
Nigris pagina crevit umbilicis.

Tibullus, iii. 1. 9–14.

Lutea sed niveum involvat membrana libellum,
    Pumex et canas tondeat ante comas;
Summaque praetexat tenuis fastigia chartae
    Indicet ut nomen littera facta meum;
Atque inter geminas pingantur cornua frontes:
    Sic etenim comptum mittere oportet opus.

Catullus, xxii. 3–8.

Idemque longe plurimos facit versus.
Puto esse ego illi millia aut decem aut plura
Perscripta, nec sic ut fit in palimpsestos
Relata; chartae regiae, novi libri,
Novi umbilici, lora rubra, membranae,
Derecta plumbo et pumice omnia aequata.

Martial, xi. 1. 1–2.

Quo tu, quo, liber otiose, tendis,
Cultus sindone non cotidiana?

Martial, iv. 10.

Dum novus est nec adhuc rasa mihi fronte libellus,
    Pagina dum tangi non bene sicca timet,
I puer, et caro perfer leve munus amico,
    Qui meruit nugas primus habere meas.
Curre, sed instructus: comitetur Punica librum
    Spongea; muneribus convenit illa meis.

Non possunt nostros multae, Faustine, liturae
Emendare iocos; una litura potest.

6. *Spongea*: note use of sponge to obliterate writing on papyrus.

Martial, x. 93. 3–6.

Perfer Atestinae nondum vulgata Sabinae
Carmina, purpurea sed modo culta toga.
Ut rosa delectat metitur quae pollice primo,
Sic nova nec mento sordida charta iuvat.

2. *Toga*: the purple-stained wrapper of the roll.
4. *Mento sordida*: i.e. dirty through the roll being rubbed against the chin.

The end of a book.

Martial, xi. 107. 1, 2.

Explicitum nobis usque ad sua cornua librum
Et quasi perlectum, Septiciane, refers.

Martial, ii. 6. 1–12.

I nunc, edere me iube libellos.
Lectis vix tibi paginis duabus
Spectas eschatocollion, Severe,
Et longas trahis oscitationes.
Haec sunt quae relegente me solebas
Rapta exscribere, sed Vitellianis.
Haec sunt singula quae sinu ferebas
Per convivia cuncta, per theatra;
Haec sunt, aut meliora, si qua nescis.
Quid prodest mihi tam macer libellus,
Nullo crassior ut sit umbilico,
Si totus tibi triduo legatur?

6. *Vitelliani*: the name of a kind of note-book.

Martial, iv. 89. 1, 2.

Ohe, iam satis est, ohe, libelle!
Iam pervenimus usque ad umbilicos.

from Latin Authors 127

A volume of epigrams can be as long or as short as the reader
likes to make it.
Martial, x. 1.

Si nimius videor seraque coronide longus
Esse liber, legito pauca: libellus ero.
Terque quaterque mihi finitur carmine parvo
Pagina: fac tibi me quam cupis esse brevem.

1. *Coronide*: the flourish which sometimes marks the end of a poem.

An epigram occupying a whole pagina or column invites the
reader to skip.
Martial, x. 59. 1, 2.

Consumpta est uno si lemmate pagina, transis,
Et breviora tibi, non meliora placent.

Yet others often have them larger.
Martial, ii. 77. 5, 6.

Disce quod ignoras: Marsi doctique Pedonis
Saepe duplex unum pagina tractat opus.

A copy with the author's autograph corrections.
Martial, vii. 17. 1–8.

Ruris bibliotheca delicati,
Vicinam videt unde lector urbem,
Inter carmina sanctiora si quis
Lascivae fuerit locus Thaliae,
Hos nido licet inseras vel imo
Septem quos tibi misimus libellos,
Auctoris calamo sui notatos.
Haec illis pretium facit litura.

A revised and enlarged edition.
Martial, x. 2. 1–4.

Festinata prior, decimi mihi cura libelli
Elapsum manibus nunc revocavit opus.

Nota leges quaedam sed lima rasa recenti;
Pars nova maior erit. Lector, utrique fave.

Use of the verso *for inferior writings.*

Martial, viii. 62.

Scribit in aversa Picens epigrammata charta,
Et dolet averso quod facit ille deo.

The fate of bad books, as waste paper.

Martial, iv. 86. 6–11.

Si te pectore, si tenebit ore,
Nec rhonchos metues maligniorum,
Nec scombris tunicas dabis molestas.
Si damnaverit, ad salariorum
Curras scrinia protinus licebit,
Inversa pueris arande charta.

Martial, iii. 2. 3–5.

Ne nigram cito raptus in culinam
Cordylas madida tegas papyro,
Vel turis piperisve sis cucullus.

Martial, vi. 61, 7, 8.

Quam multi tineas pascunt blattasque diserti
Et redimunt soli carmina docta coci.

Book-boxes.

Catullus, lxviii. 33.

Nam quod scriptorum non magna est copia apud me,
Hoc fit, quod Romae vivimus; illa domus,
Illa mihi sedes, illic mea carpitur aetas.
Huc una e multis capsula me sequitur.

Martial, xiv. 84.

Ne toga barbatos faciat vel paenula libros,
Haec abies chartis tempora longa dabit.

1. *Barbatos*: frayed, by rubbing against the dress. Hence the books
were obviously papyrus.

Reeds for pens from Egypt.

Martial, xiv. 38.

Dat chartis habiles calamos Memphitica tellus;
Texantur reliqua tecta palude tibi.

Tablets for note-books, &c.

Tibullus, iv. 7. 7, 8.

Non ego signatis quicquam mandare tabellis,
Ne legat id nemo quam meus ante, velim.

Catullus, l. 1–5.

Hesterno, Licini, die otiosi
Multum lusimus in meis tabellis,
Ut conuenerat esse delicatos.
Scribens versiculos uterque nostrum
Ludebat numero modo hoc modo illoc.

Propertius, iii. 23.

Ergo tam doctae nobis periere tabellae,
Scripta quibus pariter tot periere bona.
Has quondam nostris manibus detriverat usus,
Qui non signatas iussit habere fidem.
Illae iam sine me norant placare puellas
Et quaedam sine me verba diserta loqui.
Non illas fixum caras effecerat aurum;
Vulgari buxo sordida cera fuit.

. . . .

Me miserum! his aliquis rationem scribit avarus
Et ponit duras inter ephemeridas.

Quae si quis mihi rettulerit, donabitur auro:
Quis pro divitiis ligna retenta velit?
I, puer, et citus haec aliqua propone columna,
Et dominum Esquiliis scribe habitare tuum.

The book trade.

Martial, i. 66. 1–12.

Erras, meorum fur avare librorum,
Fieri poetam posse qui putas tanti,
Scriptura quanti constet et tomus vilis.
Non sex paratur aut decem sophos nummis.
Secreta quaere carmina et rudes curas,
Quas novit unus scrinioque signatas
Custodit ipse virginis pater chartae,
Quae trita duro non inhorruit mento.
Mutare dominum non potest liber notus.
Sed pumicata fronte si quis est nondum
Nec umbilicis cultus atque membrana,
Mercare.

4. Six to ten sesterces is a cheap copy; five denarii (see below),
an expensive one.
8. *Inhorruit*: i.e. frayed by rubbing against the chin.
11. *Membrana*: the parchment cover of a papyrus roll.

Martial, i. 117. 8–17: the poet would like his friend
to buy, not borrow, his books.

Quod quaeris propius petas licebit.
Argi nempe soles subire Letum:
Contra Caesaris est forum taberna
Scriptis postibus hinc et inde totis,
Omnes ut cito perlegas poetas.
Illinc me pete. Nec roges Atrectum
(Hoc nomen dominus gerit tabernae):
De primo dabit alterove nido
Rasum pumice purpuraque cultum
Denarîs tibi quinque Martialem.
'Tanti non es', ais? Sapis, Luperce.

Martial, iv. 72. 1, 2.

Exigis ut donem nostros tibi, Quinte, libellos.
Non habeo, sed habet bibliopola Tryphon.

Martial, i. 3. 1, 2.

Argiletanas mavis habitare tabernas,
Cum tibi, parve liber, scrinia nostra vacent.

Martial, xiii. 3.

Omnis in hoc gracili Xeniorum turba libello
Constabit nummis quattuor empta tibi.
Quattuor est nimium? Poterit constare duobus,
Et faciat lucrum bibliopola Tryphon.

Books and reading.

Propertius, iii. 9. 43–6.

Inter Callimachi sat erit placuisse libellos,
Et cecinisse modis, Coe poeta, tuis.
Haec urant pueros, haec urant scripta puellas,
Meque deum clament, et mihi sacra ferant.

Propertius, iii. 3. 17–20.

Non hic ulla tibi speranda est fama, Properti;
Mollia sunt parvis prata terenda rotis,
Ut tuus in scamno iactetur saepe libellus,
Quem legat expectans sola puella virum.

Martial, vi. 60. 1, 2.

Laudat, amat, cantat nostros mea Roma libellos,
Meque sinus omnes, me manus omnis habet.

Martial, vi. 64. 6–15.

Emendare meos, quos novit fama, libellos
Et tibi permittis felices carpere nugas:
Has, inquam, nugas, quibus aurem advertere totam
Non aspernantur proceres urbisque forique,
Quas et perpetui dignantur scrinia Sili,
Et repetit totiens facundo Regulus ore;

Quique videt propius magni certamina Circi
Laudat Aventinae vicinus Sura Dianae;
Ipse etiam tanto dominus sub pondere rerum
Non dedignatur bis terque revolvere Caesar.

Martial, xi. 3. 1–6.

Non urbana mea tantum Pimpleide gaudent
Otia, nec vacuis auribus ista damus;
Sed meus in Geticis ad Martia signa pruinis
A rigido teritur centurione liber.
Dicitur et nostros cantare Britannia versus.
Quid prodest? Nescit sacculus ista meus.

Martial, iv. 8. 7, 8.

Hora libellorum decuma est, Eupheme, meorum,
Temperat ambrosias cum tua cura dapes.

Martial, x. 19. 12, 13, 18–21.

Sed ne tempore non tuo disertam
Pulses ebria ianuam videto.

. . . .

Seras tutior ibis ad lucernas.
Haec hora est tua, cum furit Lyaeus,
Cum regnat rosa, cum madent capilli;
Tunc me vel rigidi legant Catones.

Martial's Christmas presents of books (xiv. 183–95).

183. *Homeri Batrachomyomachia.*

Perlege Maeonio cantatas carmine ranas,
Et frontem nugis solvere disce meis.

184. *Homerus in pugillaribus membranis.*

Ilias et Priami regnis inimicus Ulixes
Multiplici pariter condita pelle latent.

185. *Vergili Culex.*

Accipe facundi Culicem, studiose, Maronis,
Ne nucibus positis 'Arma virumque' legas.

186. *Vergilius in membranis.*

Quam brevis immensum cepit membrana Maronem
Ipsius vultus prima tabella gerit.

187. Μενάνδρου Θαΐς.

Hac primum iuvenum lascivos lusit amores;
Nec Glycera pueri, Thais amica fuit.

188. *Cicero in membranis.*

Si comes ista tibi fuerit membrana, putato
Carpere te longas cum Cicerone vias.

189. *Monobyblos Properti.*

Cynthia, facundi carmen iuvenale Properti,
Accepit famam; non minus ipsa dedit.

190. *Titus Livius in membranis.*

Pellibus exiguis artatur Livius ingens,
Quem mea non totum bibliotheca capit.

191. *Sallustius.*

Hic erit, ut perhibent doctorum corda virorum,
Primus Romana Crispus in historia.

192. *Ovidi Metamorphosis in membranis.*

Hic tibi multiplici quae structa est massa tabella,
Carmina Nasonis quinque decemque gerit.

193. *Tibullus.*

Ussit amatorem Nemesis lasciva Tibullum,
In tota iuvit quem nihil esse domo.

194. *Lucanus.*

Sunt quidam qui me dicunt non esse poetam;
Sed qui me vendit bibliopola putat.

195. *Catullus.*

Tantum magna suo debet Verona Catullo,
Quantum parva suo Mantua Vergilio.

INDEX

ACCENTS, in papyri, 66

Acts of the Scillitan martyrs, quoted, 63 n.

Aids to reading, lack of, in ancient books, 65–7

Alexandria, Museum and Library of, 25–7

Anaxagoras, cheap copies of, 20

Aristophanes, quoted, 22, 23

Aristophanes of Byzantium, librarian of Ptolemy Epiphanes, 88

Aristotle, library of, 25

Athenaeus, *Deipnosophistae*, 23, 29

Augustine, on use of vellum for a letter, 117

Augustus, libraries founded by, in Rome, 80

Avroman, vellum documents found at, 89

BARK, as writing material, 40

Bible, papyrus codices of, 98, 112; Vatican and Sinaitic MSS., 115

Book of the Dead, early copies of, 5

Books, form of, in relation to contents, 38; materials of, in antiquity, 16, 40 ff.

Booksellers and shops in Rome, 82

Breathings, in papyri, 66

CAESAR, Julius, form of his letters to senate, 54 n.; plans public library, 79

Caesarea, library at, 114

Callimachus, papyrus codex of, 94

Capsa, 59, 60

Cassius Hemina, on the books of Numa, 74

Catullus, descriptions of books by, 79, 124–9

Charta (= papyrus), 90 n.

Chester Beatty, A., collection of papyrus codices acquired by, 97 ff., 109

Christians, use of papyrus codex by, 95 ff.

Cicero, library of, 79

Clay, as writing material, 41

Codex, as book form, 91, 94 ff.; early use of by Christians, 95 ff.; method of formation of papyrus codices, 100 ff.;

final victory over roll form of book, 111–14

Coptic papyrus codices, quire-formation of, 107 n.; dimensions, 108

Cornua, 59

Coronis, 66

Corrections, in papyri, 71

Crete, early writing in, 7

Cumont, F., earliest vellum documents found by, 89

Cyril of Alexandria, papyrus codex of, 94, 102, 108

DEMETRIUS of Phalerum, librarian of Ptolemy I, 26

Dura, earliest vellum documents found at, 89

EGYPT, Graeco-Roman, authors read in, 32–7; origins of writing in, 4–6; Egyptian papyri, dimensions of, 47, 51

Epic Cycle, how transmitted, 14

Etruscan writing, 73, 76

Eumenes (II), of Pergamum, adoption of vellum as book material by, 87 ff.

Evans, Sir A., Cretan tablets discovered by, 7

Ezekiel, quoted, 61

FABIUS Pictor, earliest Roman chronicler, 75, 76

GADD, C. J., on early Sumerian writings, 6

Gospels, circulation of, in separate rolls and collected in codex, 99, 100; Chester Beatty papyrus of, 98

Greece, probabilities as to early knowledge of writing in, 8–15; lyric poems, tradition of, 18; reading and writing in 5th century, 19–23; lost literature of, 28–31

Grote, G., on absence of writing in Homeric age, 3, 4

HADRIAN, library founded by, in Athens, 80

Herculaneum, library discovered at, 81

CPSIA information can be obtained at www.ICGtesting.com
Printed in the USA
LVOW12s1936110414

381289LV00001B/179/A

9 781406 755596